More Praise for
Digging in the Dirt

"Home gardeners of all levels will find the information most useful. The text is simple and easy reading and full of practical, understandable information covering a broad range of timely garden topics. Highly recommended."

Dr. Lowell C. Ewart, Professor Emeritus
Department of Horticulture, Michigan State University

"Few journalists have as much gardening knowledge as writing ability ... Ed has both and offers graphic gardening advice. His comprehensive knowledge of all plant material, from trees to crocus, is obvious and enviable."

Nona Koivula, Executive Director
National Garden Bureau and All-America Selections

DIGGING IN THE DIRT
Friendly Tips for the Gardener in All of Us

By Ed Hutchison   **Second Edition**

Publisher:
From the Ground Up
4621 Congress Dr.
Midland, MI 48642

Editor:
Edward C. Hutchison

Library of Congress Catalog Number: 98-96720

ISBN: 0-9664113-1-5

Publisher's Cataloging-in-Publication
    (Provided by Quality Books, Inc.)

Hutchison, Ed (Edward Cleary), 1945-
        Digging in the dirt : friendly
        tips for the gardener in all of us /
        Ed Hutchison. -- 2nd ed.
        p. cm.
        Preassigned LCCN: 98-96720
        ISBN: 0-9664113-1-5

        1. Gardening--United States.
        I. Title.

SB453.H88 1998   635.9
                            QBI98-1336

Printed in the United States of America
Second Edition

Cover photography by Lloyd Wright
Design by AMPM, Inc.

In dedication, with thanks:

To my mother, Mary O. Hutchison, who started it all by entrusting her African violets to me as a boy of 8; to my wife, Joy, for her patience with evolving landscapes and muddy floors and to editors and readers of my weekly garden column for their probing questions, fresh perspectives and interest in my work.

Contents

Introduction 1

January

Even dormant, some perennials are glorious 2

A gentle hand gets new houseplants off to a great start . . . 4

Tired of the poinsettia? Throw it away and move on 6

Some trees, shrubs sparkle in winter landscape 8

Polish your cars, not your houseplants 10

February

Plants find snow comforting, protective 12

Sturdy houseplants laugh at dismal conditions 14

Sunshine keeps Valentine's Day plants throbbing 16

Helping houseplants through the winter blahs 18

Good stuff to think about as spring approaches 20

March

Herbs are easy from seed, productive too! 22

Warm, sunny weather fools people, not plants 24

Don't discard your Easter lily – plant it outdoors
    instead 26

Try lisianthus, lavatera and salpiglossis for
    something new 28

The friendly but strange nursery – read this
    before you go 30

April

Rabbits can be discouraged from feeding on tulips 32

Feed bulbs, trees, shrubs now ... but not lawns 34

Give soil a break: wait till it's dry to work it 36

Primrose and pansy charm the chill out of us 38

Piles of grass clippings don't have to smell bad 40

May

Leftover seeds and supplies may be okay 42

Little things early on pay off big later 44

Vigor in bedding plants counts more than pedigree 46

Now people (and birds) can enjoy sunflowers 48

Big deal in the garden ... surprise ... it's the color white . . 50

June

How to fix good things that turn bad in the yard 52

Garden not in yet? It's not too late 54

Disbudding and feeding leads to big blooms 56

Slow decomposition to stretch life of mulch 58

Plants won't go thirsty if a few conditions are met 60

July

Try bougainvillea and hibiscus for a tropical look 62

Lawns dry out quickly now, but you can help 64

Cut flowers last days longer with proper care 66

Remove obstacles to make mowing go quicker 68

Choose trees carefully to achieve years of beauty 70

Your vacation can be tough on plants back home 72

August

Headaches and joys prevail in the August garden 74

Fruit trees bear best when pollination needs are met 76

Like puppies, cute trees grow big – too big, sometimes . . . 78

September's coming – and a great time to repair
or start a lawn 80

September

Spring-flowering bulbs earn an E for Easy 82

Ferns fade in fall; color, shape and texture on hold 84

Divide narcissi for years of bountiful blooms 86

Propagating roses, amaryllis care and more 88

Chilly? So what. Keep on gardening 90

No lilies in the garden? You're missing a lot of color! 92

October

Tackle the little chores while weather's still good 94

Save time and sweat: Mow, don't rake, leaves 96

Plant trees now for a jump start next spring 98

Container plantings need extra care over winter 100

Tulips and hyacinths abound in this outdoor lasagna . . . 102

November

Look around – did pests get the best of your garden? . . . 104

Tidy up the garden before all becomes mush 106

Bulbs left to plant? Get 'em in the ground now 108

Hurry spring by forcing bulbs to bloom indoors 110

Yes, Virginia, the Christmas cactus really is a cactus 112

December

Put genetics and microclimates to your advantage 114

Harvest fresh holiday decorating materials from

    your yard 116

Sunflower seeds, fresh water spell happiness for birds . . 118

Last-minute tips to help plants survive winter 120

Go easy on food, water with houseplants 122

Entertaining kids bored during Christmas break 124

Gardening Tidbits

Tender Care for Transplants 126

Houseplants Deserve Vacation, Too 126

Three Popular Ways To Feed 127

How To Drought-Proof a Landscape 128

Tomatoes and Tubs and More 129

Getting Rid of Moss in Lawns 130

Types of Roses Defined 130

A Summer Garden in the Window Well 131

Introduction

This handbook is meant to serve as a guide to 12 months of opportunities for a nice lawn, handsome landscape, beautiful gardens and healthy houseplants. It is not meant to be a comprehensive look at any of these subjects but rather a birds-eye view of what to consider during any month of the year. My goal in preparing this handbook is the same I undertake in writing my weekly newspaper lawn and garden feature, and that is to make gardening on any level fun and rewarding.

Even dormant, some perennials are glorious

A trait some perennials share is often overlooked until now and that is the amazing amount of color they add to the winter landscape.

Seldom do gardeners choose a perennial for how it will look in winter, but it is a worthwhile selection criterion, especially if the plant is a show-stopper during summer, too.

The list of winter charmers is relatively short. Here's a peek at a few of the best, and why:

- Sedum – Unless heavy snow collapses them, the flower clusters hold up all winter. The silver-green foliage is large and fleshy and low to the ground. An excellent winter plant because its flowers are often held above snow level.

  A variety named 'Autumn Joy' is among the best because of the progressive color change the flowers undergo, beginning with light green in summer and finishing with coppery red over winter. Sedum must have well-drained soil to avoid rot over winter. Full sun or part shade.

- Iberis sempervirens – Candytuft is the common name, probably because of the clusters of bright white flowers that blanket the plant in May. The flowers are long gone now, but there's dark green foliage to admire providing snow hasn't covered it. It grows mat-like and close to the ground. Prefers well-drained, sandy soil and sun to light shade.

- Dianthus – Pinks is the common name but that's misleading because flowers can also be rose, white, salmon, yellow or shades of any of these. The evergreen foliage grows in upright tufts and can be silver, green or blue, depending on the type. The leaves resemble a grass blade but clustered. Dianthus mixes well with spring bulbs; enjoy its foliage now and the bulbs' flowers in several months. It does best in well-drained soil that is not overly rich; in other words, crummy soil is to its liking. Full sun is preferred.

- Galium odoratum – Its dried foliage and flowers were popular among the Victorians for their moth-repelling properties. Also known as sweet woodruff, it's a winter perennial noted for its aromatic green leaves that hug the ground. The aroma is more apparent in warm weather. A very fast grower, it grows best in moist, woodsy or shady places.

- Santolina chamaecyparissus – Chances are you have enjoyed its fragrant, dried foliage and flowers in wreaths and arrangements and know it by its popular name, lavender cotton. In the winter garden, this perennial is beautiful because of its blue-grey foliage that stays close to the ground. The shape of the plant resembles coral because of the way the foliage branches. It does well in average soil and full sun. While not as hardy as some perennials, it's worth a try, especially if planted in a protected area.

- Ornamental grasses – The broad, grassy, silver-green leaves of Miscanthus change to a medium tan in late autumn and maintain an attractive luster all winter long. Also known as silver banner grass, this robust perennial grows about four feet tall. Watch for its dried blades and plumes to sway gracefully in the winter breeze. Good in sun or part shade.

Many other varieties of ornamental grass also bring similar color and action to the winter garden.

When snow comes, the coppery-red color of sedum provides
a point of color in the otherwise drab winter garden.

A gentle hand gets new houseplants off to a great start

Newborns, puppies and houseplants have one thing in common and that's the uniqueness of the first few weeks in their new home.

We'll leave the care of puppies and newborns to someone knowledgeable and instead focus on new houseplants.

Many foliage houseplants are grown outdoors, under shade cloth, in Florida. Flowering houseplants such as orchids, African violets, gardenias and others are typically raised in greenhouses in a number of states. In both cases, a nurturing blend of light, growing medium, water, humidity, container, drainage and other factors are provided to produce a salable plant as quickly as possible.

While these womb-like conditions produce plants fast, they are not necessarily ideal for the plant's long-term health. This means some changes should be made soon after your plant's arrival, but more about that later.

A plant's first few weeks in your home should be quiet ones. No fertilizer. Little water. Adequate light. Isolation from other plants. Here are specifics:

- No fertilizer — Your plant needs to get used to its new surroundings before stimulants like fertilizer are provided. Besides, it has some reserves from its greenhouse days.

- Little water —Your plant will need less water than normal during this period of adjustment. Water when the top inch of the soil is dry and discard any water that remains in the saucer after 30 minutes. Depending on the humidity in your home or office, the plant may need water during this adjustment period every week or so.

- Adequate light — Place it by a bright light source, such as an east- or west-facing window. It may be happy there permanently or may need brighter light found in south exposures.

- Isolation — Keep it away from other houseplants until you are sure it is pest-free. Look for hitchhiking insects on leaves, stems, stem tips and the soil before purchasing.

This getting-to-know-you period takes two to three weeks. After that time, give the plant the care recommended on its care tag. If the tag was missing, look for details in a houseplant reference book. Excellent titles include *Crockett's Indoor Garden,* by the late James U. Crockett (Little, Brown) and *All About Houseplants,* by the editorial staff of Ortho Books (Ortho Books).

Soil-less potting mixes usually contain one or more of these ingredients: (from left) finely milled sphagnum peat moss, vermiculite or perlite.

After three weeks, consider re-potting the plant into a slightly larger container filled with a soil-less potting medium blended for houseplants. Commercial growers often use a medium that drains very fast and is very light in weight. Those are important factors when it comes to raising plants quickly, and shipping them cheaply. But the soil mix and container size may not be adequate for your plant's long term health and it's better to make the upgrades early on than run the risk of your plant languishing for months.

Tired of the poinsettia? Throw it away and move on.

You're tired of the poinsettia (won't it ever die?) and there's little extra money left after Christmas. But you'd like a fresh plant for the fresh year.

Some folks have a hard time throwing away a plant that still has life, and modern poinsettias have been bred to be full of life for a long time. Too long, in my opinion. It may live forever, or at least until Easter, even if it's ignored. Take the plunge and deep-six it in the trash or compost pile now and enjoy a new plant in your home.

A cheery choice for these grey winter days is an African violet. Today's African violet is much different from those our grandmothers raised and vastly different from those discovered 103 years ago by Baron von Saint Paul. Expert and amateur breeding has improved the shape, size, foliage, flower, color, pest resistance and overall performance of the plant.

Improvements to overall performance are appreciated by the millions of us who demand that flowering houseplants do, indeed, flower, and do so with little coaxing. Today's African violet varieties bloom more dependably than many of those bred many years ago.

If you've given up on African violets, or never tried them, now is an excellent time to give this old-fashioned plant a try. January sees a nice assortment of fresh plants arriving in supermarkets, greenhouses and similar outlets. At about $3 each, they are affordable, even with Christmas bills to pay.

Here's a review of general care tips to keep your new African violet in flower most of the year, or to awaken the flowering potential in an existing plant:

- Light – Bright, indirect light from an unobstructed north- or east-facing window is ideal. Put the plant close to the glass but not so close as to pick up the chilly air around the window. Lack of light is a prime reason why African violets quit blooming.

- Temperature – 65 to 70 degrees Fahrenheit at night with a 5 to 10 degree rise during the day. Low night temperature is another major reason why African violets quit blooming.

- Water – Add tepid water to the saucer every few days and discard any that remains after a few hours. An occasional gentle shower with the kitchen sprayer will keep leaves free of built-up grime. Use tepid water and gently pat the leaves dry with a paper towel or soft cloth. Take care not to bend the stems as they are brittle and will break easily.

- Feeding – Half-strength, water-soluble houseplant fertilizer applied once monthly from the top, rather than the bottom. Overfeeding can stifle flowering as it damages the plant's sensitive fibrous roots.

- Repotting? – If a plant wobbles in its pot, it's time for a larger container and fresh soil. Choose a pot that is about one-third the diameter of the existing plant. Example: A plant that is 12 inches across will do fine in a pot 4 inches in diameter. If the pot is too small, leaves will be damaged from drooping on the edge; too large and the roots can rot from excess moisture. Use a store-bought soil mix formulated for African violets.

To repot, carefully remove a few of the oldest leaves from the base of the plant and set the plant in the new soil at a depth that will just cover the point where the old leaves were removed. New roots will grow from this point.

- Old, tired plants – Old plants can be energized by removing the plant from the container and carefully stripping away old leaves and much of the root system and then repotting in fresh soil. It looks gruesome but is easy. For the first time, try it with someone who's done it before to help.

Old African violets can be restored to health by removing most old leaves and re-potting in fresh soil.

Some trees, shrubs sparkle in winter landscape

Just because a plant is dormant doesn't mean it has to be boring to look at.

Some, but not a lot, of trees and shrubs that are hardy where snow is a fact of winter life have at least one feature that makes them interesting in the winter.

One of my favorites is Washington hawthorne. It can be grown as a tree or shrub. I prefer the tree form and at maturity, it's about 20 feet high and about as wide. What makes it special is its clusters of bright, red, glossy berries.

Each berry is about one-quarter inch in diameter, which is on the big side for ornamental fruit. The color becomes vivid in mid-October and stays bright through winter.

This plant is very thorny, which is why I prefer to see it used in tree rather than shrub form.

A fascinating shape makes the contorted filbert interesting in winter. It has gnarled, twisting branches covered in greyish-brown bark. It is a slow-growing, compact tree best planted where its unique branching structure can be seen in winter. The common name is Harry Lauder's Walking Stick.

Some Japanese maple varieties have fascinating branch structure that can best be seen when leaves are off. 'Ever Red' and 'Crimson Queen' are among those with delicate branches arranged in whorls around the central trunk. Japanese maples grow slowly and are best used as a specimen plant in high visibility areas.

Two easy shrubs grown for their winter color are red twig and yellow twig dogwood. Red twig has cherry-red branches that grow upright, to about six feet. Yellow twig has soft, golden-yellow, upright branches and grows about as tall as its red cousin. While the bark of both remains colorful all summer, it is hidden by the medium-green foliage. Some red twig varieties have variegated pale green and white foliage.

Branches of these dogwood are most colorful when the wood is no older than three years. This is easy to control by pruning out about one-third of the old wood each year. Likewise, old and colorless red twig and yellow twig dogwoods can be energized by cutting back one-third to one-half of the branches the first year, and one-third every year after.

Eastern redbud is an attractive tree in the winter for its zig-zag branch structure and deep reddish-brown color. The branches are open, making this an ideal tree to plant near a window where some screening is wanted. The redbud is beautiful in the spring with its magenta, pea-shaped flowers that form on the trunk even before the green, heart-shaped leaves emerge.

Among other trees and shrubs that are striking in winter because of shape or color are the birches, sweet and sour gum, crabapple, holly and cotoneaster. Many gardeners favor a pin oak because the brown leaves cling all winter and its straight branches are arranged in a circular staircase fashion on the trunk.

Plant one or more of these trees and shrubs and you'll have a landscape that is as striking in the winter as it is in the summer, especially with contrast provided by the whiteness of snow.

Big, bright red berries of a hybrid crabapple look like clusters of cherries ripening in winter.

Polish your cars, not your houseplants

A deep, glossy shine is fine on cars and furniture but not on houseplants.

Despite its good looks, maintaining a glossy cosmetic shine on houseplant leaves can end up harming the plant.

Leaves of houseplants like the rubber tree, ficus, philodendron and schefflera pick up airborne dirt and grime and by doing so, their natural luster is diminished. The situation is common during winter months because the house is closed up, reducing the supply of fresh air flowing around the plant.

Over time, the build-up of dirt and grime plugs the tiny cells found on the underside of most houseplant leaves. The cells are there for breathing. And here's where the urge comes to clean the leaves.

Cleaning is a worthwhile task because it restores the natural green luster and unclogs breathing cells. A very weak soapy solution provides all the cleaning power you'll need and it does not leave behind an artificial shine. It's not as pretty, but it is more healthy.

Commercial leaf cleaning solutions are available but in my opinion, using some types may be more harmful to the plant than doing nothing. If all the solution does is clean, that's fine, but many also shine and herein is the rub. The shine is a result of a coating on the leaf surface that seems to be a magnet for dust and grime. And so the gunk layering begins anew.

Better for the plant, but more work for you, is to wipe each leaf with a solution made from one quart of warm water and a few drops of mild dishwashing soap. The soap breaks the hold the dust has on the leaf, so as it is wiped, dust is wiped away, leaving nothing behind to clog the cells.

For big plants with lots of small leaves, such as ficus, schefflera and so on, a brief shower, in the shower, gets rid of the grime. Make it a lukewarm shower and the stream a mild one. Twenty seconds should be long enough to wash the grime away. Cover the top of the container with plastic food wrap or a dry cleaning bag to keep soil from splashing out.

How often? Every four months or so is sufficient.

Houseplants with fuzzy leaves – African violets in particular – can be cleaned by gently wiping them with a soft brush. Fuzzy leaves can be occasionally rinsed with tepid water.

Clean hard-surfaced houseplant leaves with a weak solution of warm and soapy water.

Plants find snow comforting, protective

You may not like it, but plants do just fine with a deep blanket of snow.

A blanket of snow is beneficial because it protects from damage that can result from wild temperature swings over the course of a few days. Such conditions often occur at least once during winter.

For example, a forsythia is more likely to bear flowers all along its branches if it is lucky enough to be buried in snow. Buds on exposed branches are often killed by extreme cold. This explains why the nicest forsythia flowers are often found near the base of the plant.

Even snow-bound roses and tender perennials that were winterized in the autumn enjoy an added measure of protection from extreme cold and drying effects of winter winds.

Snow's effect on soil is two-fold. A continual blanket reduces the depth to which the soil freezes and this, in turn, affects when the garden can be worked and planted in the spring. Vegetable gardeners often gain two or more extra growing weeks if the soil thaws and dries out sooner because frost was not driven deeply into the ground.

Snow's other beneficial effect is to moderate the soil's temperature. This means that soil is slow to freeze and slow to thaw when snow covers it. This reduces the likelihood the top few inches of the soil will buckle during warm, sunny winter days and as a consequence, heave out shallow-rooted plants to die from the drying effects of the air.

A wet snowfall can be a nuisance when it weighs down branches of shrubs and trees. This is especially true with upright evergreens that are damaged when heavy snow grossly spreads out the branches.

Damage can be reduced if vulnerable shrubs are loosely corseted with burlap sheeting and coarse twine held in place with sturdy stakes. This task is best done in late autumn.

Branches of most evergreen shrubs are resilient enough to bounce back to their original shape as snow melts or drops away. Low branches take the brunt of heavy snowfalls and the best way to ease their burden is to gently lift and shake from underneath the branch with a broom.

Winter storms also bring ice, which is far more difficult to deal with. Ice adds enormous weight to branches of trees and shrubs and unlike snow, there is no practical way to remove it.

A blanket of snow protects rose bushes from extreme cold, which could damage the graft of the plant.

Poorly shaped trees and shrubs are most vulnerable to ice damage for the very reason they are poorly shaped – branches are plentiful but they are neither strong nor well-structured. Because there are a lot of weak branches, there's room for ice to accumulate and, because of the weight, rip the branch from the trunk.

A gardener's defense against damage from ice storms is to avoid trees and shrubs with inherently weak branches, a poor structure or both. Weeping willow and poplar come to mind as trees to avoid for this reason alone.

Another defensive move is to provide temporary support for an ice-laden branch that appears in danger of breaking. A step ladder, clothes pole or landscape timber will help.

Sturdy houseplants laugh at dismal conditions

Most houseplants will survive under the dreary growing conditions found in our homes now, but who wants a plant that merely survives? How about one that thrives instead.

Granted, some indoor gardeners provide their plants with grow lights and thrice-daily mistings. Such efforts work, as evidenced by fragrant gardenias, orchids and sturdy green plants that never drop a leaf.

If you want a nice houseplant without work, read on for a short list of foolproof houseplants and a description of each. To minimize confusion, common and botanical names are provided.

Snake plant (Sansevieria trifasciata) – The champion of no fuss. It has stiff, lance-shaped leaves that are dark green with yellow edges and horizontal bands of darker green extending down the leaves. Mature plants bear fragrant white flowers in the spring.

Jade plant (Crassula argentea) – This succulent has oblong, thick leaves one to two inches long and resembles a compact tree with a central trunk and branches. It is sometimes used for bonsai because of its pleasing shape. Bonsai or not, its compact shape can be maintained by pruning away errant branches that tend to hang down from its otherwise stiff form.

Grape ivy (Cissus rhombifolia) – Vigorous, trailing evergreen vines with dark green leaves that cover the stems. Its vigor and fullness make it an ideal hanging plant or it can be grown upright with equal success. An occasional pinching of the tips keeps it compact.

Ponytail palm (Beaucarnea recurvata) – Long, skinny leaves form a cascading arch from the trunk that looks like a big, brown onion sitting on top of the soil. An extremely tough plant with beige flowers in the summer.

Kafir lily (Clivia miniata) – Leathery, strap-like leaves about two feet tall with clusters of orange, trumpet-shaped flowers. Blooms appear in late winter and last for weeks, followed by orange-red berries. Blooms best when its roots crowd the pot so repotting is suggested only every four years or so. This plant is not as well-known as the others listed here, so you may have to hunt for it. The beautiful flowers and colorful berries make the search worth the time.

Other excellent no-fuss houseplants include members of the Peperomia species (P. sandersia, the watermelon plant), Ficus species (F. benjamina, the weeping fig), Philodendron species (P. cordatum, especially) and Aloe species.

General care is simple: Average light, stingy watering (once every week or so), a dose of houseplant fertilizer in spring and summer outdoors under a shady tree. More frequent watering may be needed in summer because the plant is likely to be growing more quickly. If repotting is needed, choose a container size slightly larger than the existing one.

Houseplants generally do best when planted in a container with drainage holes and one that is filled with a store-bought soil blended specifically for indoor plants. Some soils are quite specialized, such as for cacti or African violets. The plants listed in this article will do fine in a general houseplant soil.

The sansevieria plant takes little care, lives long and because of its vertical growth habit, is a good plant for corners. Here, Joan Schrott, a Michigan florist, grooms a sansevieria.

Sunshine keeps Valentine's Day plants throbbing

Don't blame your Valentine if that beautiful gardenia plant you received has quit blooming already.

Instead, chalk it up as a thoughtful gift, but curses on the houseplant industry for tempting us with this oh-so-fussy but beautiful plant.

Gardenia blossoms are lovely because of their waxy, white color and rich fragrance. And the leaves are a rich, dark, glossy green. While leaves aren't a problem to maintain, flowering will stop unless all conditions indoors are right, and they seldom are in our homes over winter.

Here's hoping you got an easier plant and if so, here's how to care for it:

Lots of sunshine is your best ally. It keeps the plant flowering longer by helping flower buds in various stages of development open fully. Sunshine keeps the leaves healthy and busy making food for more flowers and leaves. And it keeps the plant bushy and not reaching for light.

Flowering plants tend to need more water than those with just green leaves, and some of those sold around Valentine's Day are especially thirsty.

The azalea with its clear pink, rose, white or bicolor flowers is one. Florist azaleas are raised in lightweight soil that dries out evenly and quickly. Check it daily and water if the surface feels dry.

The hibiscus also needs frequent watering to meet the needs of its woody stems and large leaves. This is a born-again plant and many people aren't familiar with its care but are attracted to its big (four-inch) blooms in shades of pink, yellow and orange. Blooms last just one day but a heavily budded and cared-for plant will bloom for two or more weeks. Add water when the soil surface dries out.

Cyclamens get by with less water, but among the bunch, have the deepest craving for a sunny window. Scratch the soil and if it is dry fingertip deep, give it a drink. Cool temperatures and lots of light will keep a cyclamen blooming for several weeks. Day temps of 60 and evenings of 50s are ideal.

The kalanchoe is another popular Valentine's Day plant that scoffs at frequent watering. Because it is a succulent, it stores water in its thick, fleshy leaves and needs water only when the soil is dry to the touch two or so inches deep. Go very easy on watering. Too much water and its chunky stem will rot at the base and one morning, you'll find the top has crashed to the floor. If leaves yellow, it is probably a sign of overwatering and the chance for recovery is next to none.

The Jerusalem cherry has a similar thirst as the cyclamen and likes the same cool, sunny spot.

When watering these and other plants, do so until water drains out the bottom of the container. Discard whatever water is left standing in the saucer after 15 minutes.

What's great about these plants – azalea, cyclamen, kalanchoe, hibiscus and Jerusalem cherry – is they ask so little and bloom so well for so long.

Hibiscus flowers are huge and colorful and the plant requires little care to keep 'em coming.

Helping houseplants through the winter blahs

Even though winter is on the wane, some houseplants may be struggling with the stress of life indoors.

Many houseplants trace their origins to the tropics and while we can mist 'em and light 'em to our heart's content, conditions indoors could hardly be described as tropical.

Fortunately, simple changes such as misting, moving the plant closer to a sunny window or finding it a warmer location can make a big difference in its health.

Here's a look at a few popular houseplants and the kind of symptoms they may be displaying now, the probable cause and what you can do to help.

Boston fern – Few new leaves form and the youngest leaves turn yellow and crinkly while the plant takes on a wiry appearance and shrinks. Cause: Too little humidity. Mist the plant twice daily or move it to a sunny, moist room, such as the kitchen or laundry room.

Swedish ivy – Leaves turn pale green; oldest leaves yellow and drop off. Cause: Nutrients in the soil have been depleted, a common problem with rapidly growing houseplants such as Swedish ivy. Feed the plant monthly with a general purpose houseplant fertilizer.

Dracaena – Leaves grow larger than normal and turn deep green and are stiff; older foliage yellows and falls away. Cause: Too much fertilizer. Run water through the soil for several minutes to leach out fertilizer salts. Replace the top several inches of soil and stop feeding until it recovers, then feed sparingly.

Sansevieria – New growth stops and existing foliage turns dark green and eventually becomes mushy. Cause: Excess water and fertilizer. Reduce water and food if only a few leaves are affected and snip away the bad leaves. Discard the plant if more than half of the leaves show signs of decay.

Dieffenbachia – Variegated leaves turn yellow, then tan or brown, curl and may develop red edges along the margin. Cause: A sudden change in light, probably from low to high levels, is disrupting production of chlorophyll and bleaching the leaf tissue. Reduce light but keep the soil evenly moist.

African violet – Leaves curl down and around themselves and older leaves take on a purplish tint. Cause: The plant is cold. It does best when temperatures are constant between 65 and 75 degrees. Move it to a warmer room.

Dieffenbachia leaves lighten when exposed to excess light. Some varieties (shown) have lighter leaves to begin with and these tend to fare better under stronger light.

Good stuff to think about as spring approaches

Are people anxious for spring? You bet they are, if questions that come my way in February are a sign of enthusiasm for the season just ahead. Folks are eager to get outdoors and enjoy golf, cookouts, after-dinner walks and, yes, even yard chores.

Here is a snapshot look at what is often on people's minds with the official start of spring about one month away:

Q: Can I put fertilizer on the lawn now so it's there when the grass starts growing?

A: Late winter feeding is not advisable because it will force the grass to grow at an unhealthy, rapid rate when the weather breaks. It also means you'll be mowing at least twice a week. A healthy, established lawn that was fertilized in the fall should not be fed again until mid-May. It's okay to feed weak or new lawns a few weeks earlier.

The only benefit of applying fertilizer now is that it's one less thing to do in the spring. On balance, it's best to wait until the time that's best for your lawn — not the time that's convenient for you.

Q: Is a soil test worthwhile?

A: Absolutely, especially if you are starting a new lawn or garden this spring or if either your garden or lawn did poorly last year. One of the best consumer values around is the inexpensive but thorough soil test many land grant universities offer through county cooperative extension offices.

A test will provide an understanding of what you can expect from your soil and how you can improve it. Without that knowledge, you may be wasting effort and money in working fertilizer and amendments into the soil. Check with your local extension office for details; chances are, the test can be run in early spring after frost has disappeared and the soil has dried out a bit.

About $75 and a few hours labor are sufficient to take care of your lawn's weed and feed needs for the season. As with any lawn and garden fertilizer or chemical, it's always a good idea to read and heed instructions on the label.

Q: Should I sign up for a lawn care program?

A: Perhaps. If you don't want to be bothered with feeding, weeding and watching for pests, or can't do these things by yourself, then a lawn care company may be the answer.

Don't expect a service to work quick miracles. If your lawn is a mess, it will take at least two years to turn it around. And if you contract with a service, follow their advice as it relates to mowing and watering and call them the instant you spot problems or become dissatisfied. Be interested in what they say and ask as many questions as necessary to gain a complete understanding of what they want to do, why, how much it will cost and the benefit you can expect from the service.

That said, my experience has been that about $75 and your labor will buy all the fertilizer and weed killer you'll need to keep a 10,000-square foot lawn in tiptop shape for the year.

Q: What about tree and shrub services these companies provide?

A: My experience, and from what I've heard from other gardeners, is that their appraisals of the health of trees and shrubs is often unduly pessimistic and that more service is recommended than is really needed. This is not to say their service is not warranted. Ask questions to learn what's really needed. And don't try to get rid of every insect around; it's neither possible nor advisable despite an arsenal of chemistry available to do combat.

Spraying trees taller than 15 feet is best done by a professional equipped with equipment that reaches high into the uppermost branches. There are two times of the year when doing so is important – early spring to kill eggs before they hatch and again in early summer to get rid of fresh insects that feed on leaves. An alternative to spraying is the use of systemic insecticide "caps" that are placed under the bark of the tree by first drilling a small hole in the trunk.

Q: What are some good trees to plant?

A: The list is long enough to offer lots of choice, but it's not an endless list. Two excellent local resources are the professionals at a local nursery or your city forester. The criteria that urban foresters use to choose among hundreds of types of trees will usually apply to homeowners, too.

Chances are, you are after a tree that has a nice, broad crown (top) but not one that is massive; a tree that doesn't splinter in ice- or windstorms; one that has pretty fall color; one that doesn't break up the sidewalks nor get in the sewer or septic fields; one that isn't attractive to bugs and disease and in general, is trouble-free, grows moderately fast and is beautiful year-around.

So what are they? New or seldom-used varieties of elm, maple, European beech, flowering dogwood, serviceberry, crabapple and insect-tolerant birch may be just right for you. Expect trade-offs and wherever possible, choose a variety that is attractive in some fashion through the seasons.

Herbs are easy from seed, productive too!

There's still time to start herbs indoors and enjoy a few sprigs of their foliage before setting the plants outdoors when danger of frost has past.

Two factors make this possible. Day length has increased to the point plants can get enough natural light to thrive, or artificial light is easy to arrange. The other factor is that some of the most useful herbs from a culinary perspective do just fine indoors.

While my experience with herbs indoors has been successful, it is limited, so I turned to an expert for advice on what and how to grow it indoors. Donna Frawley, a Michigan herb expert and retailer of herbs and related products, provided the details.

She said that chives, basil, oregano, rosemary, thyme, mint and lemon balm are easy to grow indoors.

"Basil is one of the easiest herbs to grow indoors," she said. "It is also one of the most versatile. It is used a lot to add flavor and color to pasta, chicken and similar dishes popular among health-conscious consumers. It is also a wonderful 'topper' sprinkled on fresh vegetables and salads."

For soil, Frawley recommends a lightweight, store-bought mix that may be a blend of things like peat, perlite, vermiculite and similar non-soil components. Or, you can use a mix that contains part real soil. The important thing is that it is an airy mix so water will drain quickly, she noted.

Because regular potting soil is on the heavy side, it has a tendency to stay wet too long for the fine roots of herb plants. A mix labeled as suitable for starting seed or growing African violets will be fine for herbs.

Herbs grown in a soil-less medium should be fertilized lightly, perhaps every six weeks, with a water-soluble food mixed at half-strength. Plants grown in a mix that includes some soil won't need fertilizer, she said. Too much fertilizer leads to lush foliage at the loss of production of the oil that gives the particular herb its distinctive flavor.

Frawley grows her herbs under artificial light, using standard four-foot fluorescent fixtures outfitted with grow-light bulbs. She recommends the tubes be positioned about six inches from the top of the plant and be turned on 12 to 16 hours daily.

Herb plants are easy to raise from seed and, if started in early March, will be big enough to harvest some leaves before it's time to set the plants out in the garden.

Virtually any container is fine, providing it has drainage holes. One of her favorites for sprouting seeds is a half-gallon waxed-type paper milk carton, cut lengthwise. It provides plenty of depth for the roots and is a convenient size for fitting under the fluorescent lights. Most herb seeds are fine and should be carefully sprinkled on the surface. Most will sprout within 10 to 15 days, or sooner if they are coaxed along with bottom heat.

"Growing herbs indoors is really fun," she said. "You'll be amazed how good an herb tastes without having to open a store-bought spice jar."

Warm, sunny weather fools people, not plants

If a run of warm and sunny weather is enough to coax people out of their dormant state, what about plants?

Here are two reasons not to worry about plants sprouting too soon because of early warmth: They probably won't and even if they do, little can be done about it.

Sometimes, there are very early springs that fool plants into growing too soon only to zap them in April with a hard freeze. That condition is more a concern for orchardists who face the loss of a crop if frost comes at the wrong time.

For the most part, the rest of us can sit back, relax and enjoy the sunshine, if and when it comes.

The two key factors that waken a tree or woody shrub from winter dormancy are day length and temperature. That days are getting longer and warmer has already triggered activity in the plant. Roots are beginning to take up ground water and sap is flowing and this causes leaf and flower buds to swell.

A few days of very nice weather are seldom enough, though, to push the plant further than it should be at this time of year.

Problems can develop when there is a sudden and dramatic drop in temperature, say, from 60 degrees at noon to 10 degrees at 9 p.m. Such a drop can damage tender buds in mid-March as well as mid-April. What typically happens is that days are warm and the temperature gradually drops to the mid-20s at nightfall. This presents no problem.

Even if an extreme drop occurred and buds were frozen, a healthy tree or shrub will recover and send out a new flush of leaf buds. Flower buds on shrubs or fruit trees, however, would be lost until next season. A weak plant without reserve energy would likely die or be severely stunted.

The healthy plant that makes it through such an ordeal would need special care during the growing season to help it build back its reserves. Watering, feeding and insect control become much more important.

Too, there is no need to worry about bulb plants that sprout early. There will be little sustained growth and flowering until the plant has all the warmth it needs.

The exception is with bulbs planted near buildings where temperatures are warmer. These will develop quicker than those in garden beds and may be harmed by deep freezes. A protective blanket of straw will help them through the coldest nights.

Gardeners with roses protected by foam cones would do well to open the base gradually for fresh, cool air, especially during a prolonged warm spell. If the cone has a removable top, take it off so the air inside will stay naturally cool. The greenhouse effect of cones can force a rose bush to start growth much too soon. That is the major drawback of using cones for protection – it heats up quickly and retains heat too long. Mounding soil around the base of rose bushes in the fall eliminates the greenhouse effect.

Rhododendron leaves perk up when temperatures climb. Even though the flower buds are plump, they won't open until it's time.

Don't discard your Easter lily – plant it outdoors instead

The Easter lily is one of the few florist crops that can be transplanted outdoors where it will thrive and bloom for many years.

Unlike poinsettias, cyclamens, azaleas and other florist crops that require coaxing to get more flowers, the Easter lily reblooms effortlessly. Here's how to go about it:

Remove flowers as they wilt and when they are all gone, move the plant to a sunny window. Water it when the soil feels dry to the touch, but not so much that the soil's soggy or that water is standing in the saucer. Feed it every six weeks with a half-strength solution of houseplant fertilizer. This will help maintain its foliage and build the bulb's strength for another blooming cycle.

Plant the bulb outdoors about May 15 in a spot that gets a lot of sun and where the soil is rich and well-drained. If the native soil has a lot of clay or sand, mix one part compost or sphagnum peat moss to three parts soil in the planting hole.

If you are adventuresome, gently remove the plant from the pot and brush away soil from the bulb. The bulb should be planted about six inches deep, measured from its tip to the soil surface. Or, you may find it easier to remove the entire plant intact from the container. It still gets planted at the same depth, six inches, which will replicate the depth it was growing in while in the pot.

In mid-May the top is usually still green and healthy. Don't cut if off. Spread a two-inch layer of mulch around the area to keep the bulb's roots cool, a condition it favors.

After a few weeks outdoors, the top will wither and it can then be removed. New growth will emerge a few weeks later. Easter lilies normally bloom in early summer and the bulb may bloom again its first year in your garden.

Chances are the foliage will top out without flower buds. The foliage, though, will spend the summer making food that will help the bulb rebuild its energy for blossoms next year. After it gets established and its easy needs for sun are met, the bulb should be all set to re-bloom each June.

While the bulb is hardy over winter, it is still a good idea to protect it with a mulch of pine needles, chopped-up leaves, shredded bark or something similar.

Like most plants, the Easter lily has some interesting history behind it. For example, the potted Easter lily is an American and Canadian curiosity when it comes to florist products. Europeans and Japanese enjoy their Easter lilies as cut blossoms in early summer, the normal blooming period for the plant.

Unpot a lily and you'll find a bulb made up of overlapping, succulent scales. Since World War II, it's been a product of American horticulture. The Japanese controlled the market until that point. Now, the U.S. and Canadian market is serviced by 10 growers located on a narrow coastal band from Brookings, Ore., to Smith River, Calif. It takes three years to produce a lily bulb.

For commercial growers, the forcing process begins in October when bulbs arrive from the Pacific Northwest fields. They are potted in a loamy, lightweight soil. Rooting begins almost immediately and continues for two weeks, after which winter begins. Their winter is a six-week period in a cooler, with temperatures held at 45 degrees. This cold period is necessary for the flower, already formed in the bulb, to develop properly.

Out of the cooler, there are 110 days on the greenhouse bench. The growing continues at about an inch a week. Virtually all lilies are bought by consumers in a short period, beginning just before Palm Sunday and continuing through Easter Sunday.

Ten growers in Oregon and California annually raise some 12 million Easter lily bulbs that are sold to local growers to raise as plants for Easter.
(Photo courtesy Easter Lily Research Foundation)

Try lisianthus, lavatera and salpiglossis for something new

If you have an urge to try something unusual in your flower garden this year, look to the "l, l and s" team.

"L, l and s" is my term for three annuals that are seldom found as bedding plants. That's because consumers aren't clamoring for them and the bedding plant industry has other things that are easier to grow and more popular with consumers.

"L, l and s" stands for lisianthus, lavatera and salpiglossis. Despite inherent flaws, each is a summer charmer and is a great change of pace from the familiar summer trilogy of petunia-zinnia-marigold.

I have either grown or monitored field trails of each and heartily recommend them. Since they are hard to find as bedding plants, I'll start seeds in my basement, under light, for transplants ready to go mid-May. Here are a few details on each.

Lisianthus answers to a few names. Texans call it Prairie Gentian; some botanists call it Eustoma. It is a wildflower in the Southeast and in the last few years has received some breeding attention in Holland and Japan. It grows 18 to 24 inches tall with waxy, silver-green foliage and bears flowers at the tip of short stems.

The plant itself is not attractive but the flowers are stunning. They look like a rose blossom, frozen as petals are unfolding. Blossoms are very clear shades of white, pink and lavender. As a cut flower, blooms last two weeks – hard to beat that!

Lisianthus is happiest in areas of the United States where days are genuinely hot, day after day. The plant tends to be stringy with little side growth. What is appealing and makes it worthwhile for even the smallest garden is the flower. The soft colors are clean and crisp, and they last so long on the plant or as cut flowers that the plant itself becomes secondary.

Lavatera is an old-fashioned plant that is popular in Europe where it is known as Tree Mallow. It has been available in the United States for several years. Varieties are limited with 'Silver Cup,' 'Mont Blanc' and 'Mont Rose' most often available.

The plant grows about two feet tall with large, open flowers that look like hibiscus blossoms. The pink or white color is soft and clear. I saw 'Silver Cup' and 'Mont Blanc' grow side by side and was impressed with how the flowers covered the plant, making it almost glow, even in bright sun.

Its shape, size and flowering habits make it an unusual plant. It has the height of a zinnia or marigold and the blooming free-for-all of a petunia – and that's an unusual combination in the annual garden. It is easy to grow from seed, but since the plant doesn't like its roots disturbed, start the seed in Jiffy peat pots or peat pellets.

The shape, color and long life of the lisianthus blossom make it a worthwhile garden annual, even though the plant itself is not attractive.

Salpiglossis has petunia-like flowers with heavy veining on the petals, like someone has taken a paint brush and traced fine lines. 'Friendship' and 'Casino' are two popular varieties, although selection will vary depending on where you find seed. Colors tend to run in the reds, oranges and rose shades. It likes cool nights.

Salpiglossis isn't likely to be available as transplants, but it starts easily from seed. Like lavatera, it is not yet a substitute for a bed of petunias or marigolds, but has something different to offer in its deeply veined flowers. If you can find lisianthus as a plant, do so, as it takes three to four months to bloom from seed.

Check seed racks at local stores or one of these mail-order firms: Park Seed Co., Greenwood, SC 29647-0001; Thompson & Morgan, P.O. Box 1308, Jackson, NJ 08527; and W. Atlee Burpee & Co., Warminster, PA 18974. Each company offers a free catalog.

The friendly but strange nursery – read this before you go

Countless folks in search of a new plant will soon venture into a jungle teeming with strange sights, sounds and smells.

The jungle is the plant nursery and in a few weeks, area nurseries will be stocked with fresh trees and shrubs, herbicides, fungicides, insecticides and other botanical, chemical and mechanical wizardry that hold the potential to make great horticultural things happen in your backyard.

Here are some tips to get the most from this season's forays to your favorite nursery.

The sounds – Nurserymen mix English and Latin in their speech, much to the consternation of many customers, such as:

"Hey Sam, this guy wants a Quercus palustris delivered Monday. Can we do it?" shouts one nurseryman to the other.

"Nope, we're outta palustris, but we got some nice alba" is the reply.

Pity the customer. He had just asked for a shade tree that would live a long time and bear rich, green summer foliage and good autumn color. It was a pin oak (Quercus palustris) but alas, all the nursery had available was a white oak (Quercus alba).

An oak is not an oak and indeed, there's a big difference between a white oak and a pin oak, as there is among the other common oaks: Sawtooth, shingle, bur, chinkapin, chestnut, English and red, to name just a few.

While the dialog can be troubling, nurserymen who talk in mixed tongues do so to precisely identify a given plant. The plant's botanical name (Latin) is widely accepted by nurserymen throughout the world. It's somewhat like ordering a Big Mac at McDonald's in Chicago or Moscow and knowing it's going to be the same sandwich in either place.

Read plant labels when shopping. Most will give the correct botanical name, followed by the variety name or common name. Ask the nurseryman about differences because it may not be apparent on the label.

Don't think that a high-sounding botanical name guarantees a plant is special, or even worthwhile. Betula pendula may look impressive on a tag, but it is merely the botanical name for European white birch, a short-lived, insect-ridden tree that's destined to be disappointing. Ditto for Populus alba. It's the name for white poplar, a tree that is favored by at least 16 different and troublesome insects and diseases.

The sights – Some are encouraging: An azalea or rhododendron loaded with fat flower buds just beginning to show color while others are perplexing, such as a bundle of sticks stuck in a plastic tub filled with soil.

Whatever the plant, bear in mind that it was probably dug a few weeks ago or maybe late last fall from a growing field a few or thousands of miles distant and shipped to the nursery. No matter how beautiful or pitiful the plant looks now, rest assured that with proper care its appearance and value will improve each year.

The smells – Shredded or chipped bark sold for mulch in bags or bulk will have a pleasant, moist, woodsy fragrance. Bark that is trucked to the nursery and sold in bulk (usually by the yard) is usually much less expensive than similar material sold bagged. Ask your nurseryman's advice for what's right for your situation. Inquire about color, texture, longevity and if there's a need to add nitrogen to the soil. When some barks decompose, the nitrogen level gets out of kilter and the imbalance can cause some plants to grow poorly.

The promises – Most nurseries offer a plant guarantee of some sort, which is admirable considering the firm has no control once the plant leaves the premises. Guarantees are a sign of a nurseryman's confidence in the plant's health, its adaptability to local conditions and his customers' good will in planting and caring for it properly.

Ask specifics: How long is the guarantee in effect? Should the plant fail, will it be replaced at no cost to the customer? Half price? Replaced with a similar specimen, but no cash refund? Does the guarantee apply to stock planted only by the nursery? Does it apply to sale merchandise? What if the label says the rose is red and it instead blossoms white? And so on. Should a plant die, most nurseries want to see the dead plant. Their desire is not to verify that it's dead, but to help the staff understand what went wrong.

The other stuff – Nurseries tend to stock plenty of lawn and garden chemicals to correct soil conditions, insects and disease typical to a given locale. This depth of product knowledge is worth the slightly higher price a jar of whatever costs at the nursery versus a nearby discount store.

Nurserymen will quote plants by their botanical names. Read up on them in any good gardening book before shopping.

Rabbits can be discouraged from feeding on tulips

You like a fresh salad and so do rabbits. That's why the poking-through-the-soil tips of crocus and tulips are at risk.

Now's the time to minimize the risk. More about how to do that in a moment.

The tender tips are like a fresh salad to rabbits. One rabbit can chomp through dozens in no time. The result is a nourished, happy rabbit but no flowers.

The rabbit's meal essentially stops the bulb from carrying out its mission to flower and reproduce. The rabbit does not have to eat the flower bud to stop its development. Mowing down the bulb's tip is enough.

The tip is most vulnerable when it's about two inches high and growing rapidly. For crocus and some tulips, that usually occurs in early April. This is before grass or weeds begin growing so fresh greens are scarce in the neighborhood. Hyacinths come up later in the season when other greens are available so they are not as vulnerable. For some reason, rabbits don't feed on daffodil tips.

So, how do you discourage rabbits from making your bulb plantings a salad bowl?

In my experience, the best way is to make the tips taste awful to the rabbit, without hurting the tip, or the rabbit. A product called Ro-Pel (Burlington Scientific Corp., Farmingdale, N.Y.) does just that.

The product's been on the market for years. I think it is over-priced, but it does do the job of discouraging rabbits from feeding on foliage. It is sold in a plastic bottle, ready to spray on the foliage.

Once applied, the material dries and remains on guard for several days, unless a heavy rain washes it away. The rabbit nibbles on treated tips and apparently finds the taste quite awful. So the rabbit hops to the next tip and has the same experience and goes away. It may return several times and if the same taste is encountered, I guess there is some learning involved and it eventually decides to stay away.

I don't know what the stuff tastes like to a rabbit but I accidentally tasted it and found it vile, strong and lasting. I applied it one year without wearing gloves and some of the mist settled on my fingers. Later, even after washing my hands, I discovered the taste while eating potato chips.

Other materials are available and some discourage rabbits by smell rather than taste. If you use any of these materials, please wear gloves and to be on the safe side, eye protection. I am a big fan of wearing protective gear when using any garden chemical, even if the label does not say to do so.

Other ways to discourage rabbits: Some folks sprinkle human hair or dried blood meal in the area as a repellent. Others crisscross two pieces of chicken wire over the bed to make it difficult for rabbits to feed. I've had excellent luck with Ro-Pel and will continue to use it.

Whatever you choose, keep an eye on your bulb plantings and put the protection in place before rabbits begin their feast.

Look closely. The tip of this tulip has been mowed down by a rabbit. It will not flower as a result.

Feed bulbs, trees, shrubs now ... but not lawns

Now is a great time to feed bulbs, trees and shrubs, but not the grass.

Why early spring? It is because these plants can use a boost of energy now, just as the new growing season begins.

And why not feed lawns? Feeding a healthy lawn now forces top growth, at the expense of root development. That means roots suffer and so will you because the grass will need cutting all the time.

At this time of the year, solid rather than liquid, plant food seems more effective since there is little (or no) foliage to take in the nutrients for transport to the roots. Even so, if the liquid fertilizer is applied to the soil around the bulbs, the nutrients will eventually work their way to the root zone.

Sprinkling granular fertilizer around emerging bulb foliage is the way I like to go about feeding daffodils, crocus, tulips and other spring bulbs. A handful of fertilizer for every 12 bulbs is a reasonable measure. The fertilizer will go to work more quickly if it's worked into the top inch of soil. A garden fork or similar hand tool that lets you maneuver around the bulb tips works well. To avoid burning foliage, wash away any fertilizer that is accidentally sprinkled on it.

For trees and shrubs, I prefer solid fertilizer spikes that are pounded into the soil at the outer edge of the plant. I like spikes because they are inexpensive, accurate and easy to use. The rule of thumb is one spike for every inch diameter of the plant trunk, but follow the package instructions to be sure.

You can also use a root feeder, although the task will take more time than it does with spikes because each of the fertilizer tablets will take several minutes to dissolve. The one advantage of the root feeder is it puts the fertilizer in solution and makes it immediately available to the plant. Another technique is to work granular fertilizer into the soil surrounding trees and shrubs. Ideally there's mulch or soil rather than grass in these areas. How much fertilizer is needed depends on the size of the tree or shrub; check the label to be sure.

For large trees planted in grassy areas, some folks apply tree fertilizer with their lawn spreader, dispensing the material near the drip line of the tree. The drip line is the point at which the outermost branches would touch the soil and is where many of the feeder roots are found.

Various fertilizer formulations are available to meet the needs of different trees and shrubs. The major groups include blends for acid-loving plants, evergreens, fruit trees, flowering shrubs and roses. The difference is mostly in the amount of nitrogen, phosphorous and potassium (NPK). If it is not practical for you to purchase and store several types of fertilizer, then use a general purpose fertilizer that contains a somewhat even blend of NPK.

Early spring feeding makes sense for another reason and that is that fertilizer applied mid-summer can trigger growth that does not mature before cold weather returns in fall. While grass reacts quickly to the presence of fertilizer, trees and shrubs may take a few months to acknowledge the feeding with better color or a spurt of new growth.

Back to lawns. If your lawn is in reasonable shape, it is better to let warm weather and existing nutrients in the soil green it gradually. Healthy lawns are best fed for the first time in mid-May. Lawns that are thin because they are new or have been neglected will benefit from an April feeding and additional feedings on Memorial Day, July 4, Labor Day and Halloween. The Halloween feeding should be with a fall-type fertilizer.

Fertilizer applied around emerging bulb foliage helps create next year's flowers, especially on daffodils.

Give soil a break: wait till it's dry to work it

A word of advice to eager-beavers ready to prepare the soil for planting: Wait.

This time of the year, garden soil is typically wet because of rainfall and frost working its way out. It is too wet to work.

Power tilling or hand digging of wet soil often results in lumpy soil as the soil mass dries. This happens because the various components of the soil cannot properly blend with each other when disturbed in a wet state. Clay often is brought to the surface and its particles cling to form lumps that dry very hard.

From a spring moisture perspective, soil can be safely worked when a fistful makes a ball that crumbles when pressure is released. If it stays in a ball, that usually means it is either too wet or has a lot of clay.

How long it takes to dry before it is safe to work depends on depth of the frost, amount of rain, exposure to sunlight, temperature and the composition of the soil. Sandy soils will dry out more quickly than those with a lot of clay. Waiting just two weeks can make a huge difference in the "workability" of the spring soil.

What you can do now is get the soil tested to see what the soil is lacking and what can be done to improve it.

As we go merrily on our gardening way, we often forget that soil quality degrades over time. Weathering and the plants' use of nutrients from it takes a toll and eventually there is a noticeable difference in how well things grow in the garden.

Because degradation is usually gradual, a homeowner does not see striking differences from one year to the next. A decline in plant performance can often be traced to soil that has also declined. This decline is often in the level of nutrients (nitrogen, phosphorous, potassium) and micronutrients in the soil. Sometimes the level of soil acidity, as noted by a pH reading, changes and the change also adversely affects plants' performance.

Soil test kits can be purchased at nurseries and home centers. However, I recommend that a professional test be done every five years, rather than rely on home kits. If you enjoy gardening and are putting time, effort and money into it, the stakes are too high not to get a professional review of your soil. Often, county extension agents can arrange for an inexpensive but very thorough test for you.

Some professional tests do not include a check for pH level. This is a fairly easy test and do-it-yourself kits that are reliable and inexpensive are available at nurseries and home centers.

As you consider your soil's health, also think through its structure – basically, how friendly is it to the plants that call it home. The structure, too, can change over time.

Wait until soil dries before tilling or deep digging it.

A soil with a lot of clay, or sand, or one that seems worked out, can be improved by working in compost, sphagnum peat moss or a similar organic matter on a regular basis. This is not practical for an established lawn but is a task easily done on a garden plot.

Probably the best time of year to work in soil amendments is early in the fall, just after frost has zapped the plants. This is a good time because the amendments will begin to break down and as they do, gradually improve the soil structure. Don't wait too late in the fall to work this material in as its speed of decomposition depends on the warmth of the soil.

Fairly large quantities of organic matter are needed to make a difference in the soil structure. As a rough guideline, consider working in a two inch blanket of compost or sphagnum peat moss or a six inch layer of fallen leaves into the top six inches of the soil every autumn. This quantity and frequency will go a long way in making the soil a friendly place for plants' roots to grow and prosper.

Primrose and pansy charm the chill out of us

While frost is likely for several more weeks, it is safe to plant two of spring's most charming plants – primrose and pansy.

Unlike impatiens, geraniums and other summer flowers, pansies and primroses like the cool weather of spring. They dislike summer heat and quit blooming when it comes.

Both bear colorful, bright flowers on bushy, compact plants. Primrose blossoms are about one inch across; most pansy varieties bear larger flowers up to three inches across. Primrose flowers are usually a solid, clear color while pansies can be solid or blotched. Neither is particularly fragrant.

Besides a passion for cool weather, they share a taste for soil that is rich and well-drained. A layer of mulch around the base of the plant helps keep the soil cool and moist, which is also to their liking. Primroses prefer partial shade while pansies prefer mostly sun.

These are compact plants, seldom exceeding 8 to 12 inches high. They look best when planted in clusters, rather than strung out single file. Pansies get bushy, so they are good when a lot of them are massed in a bed. Primroses spread, too, but not as much as pansies and are best used as a border plant.

Feed once a year with a granular fertilizer worked into the soil in the spring. Or, give them a foliar feeding twice a year, in the spring and early autumn.

Their flowers are so bright that even a few plants will liven a dull area. Sandy or heavy clay soil is easily fixed to their liking by blending equal parts of sphagnum peat moss or compost with the native soil to a depth of eight inches. Fixing the immediate planting area is all that's needed.

For an area the size of a card table, this will take about 15 minutes. Simply dump the peat moss or compost on the top of the spot and work it in with a shovel or tiller. Garden centers sell bagged sphagnum peat moss (the dry stuff in the tightly packed bales) and packaged compost.

Keep the soil moist – spring rains usually do this for you – and the plants will keep putting out bright flowers until the weather turns hot in June. Neither blooms well over summer but will resume blooming when cool weather returns in September and will keep at it through October.

While both will spread by self-seeding, clumps of primrose should be divided every three years to maintain their vigor. Both are hardy over winter, especially when protected by a blanket of snow or a light cover of mulch.

Look for pansies and primroses wherever garden plants are sold. Pansies are usually sold in cell packs and primrose as single, potted plants. Primroses are the more expensive of the two.

A yellow primrose is an especially welcome
sight on a dreary spring day.

Piles of grass clippings don't have to smell bad

Pretty soon, the unmistakable stench of rotting grass will assault the nose of anyone in close range of, or downwind from, an ill-kept compost pile.

The ban on lawn waste in public landfills is forcing homeowners to be resourceful in how they get rid of grass clippings. For many, it means dumping them in the back corner of the yard and hoping for the best. Others take a more deliberate approach and pile the clippings uniformly. From careful piles, there's seldom a smell and usually rich compost develops as a result of the process of decomposition.

The best way to avoid the scourge of a smelly compost pile made from grass clippings is to avoid bagging the clippings in the first place. Clippings left on the lawn return valuable nutrients to the food chain and do not contribute to thatch buildup. Still, many homeowners bag clippings, especially in the spring and fall when grass is growing fast.

Here's a review of what smells are common in compost piles and what to do to achieve an odor-free and effective pile. Please consider this article as a quick once-over on composting, especially as it relates to managing grass clippings in the spring and autumn.

An ammonia smell coming from the pile means that it is overloaded with materials high in nitrogen, such as grass clippings. By adding carbon-containing materials such as straw, leaves or hay, the imbalance is corrected and decomposition, without smells, resumes.

A rotting, pungent odor means that the material is rotting rather than decomposing. There's a big difference to the nose. A decomposition smell is earthy and light while a rotting one is heavy and offensive. Rotting smells are common when a bulk of dense, wet materials (like grass clippings) are heaped in the corner of a yard.

A primary reason piles rot rather than decompose is a shortage of oxygen for the microorganisms that do the work. The solution: Introduce oxygen by stirring the pile, turning over the various layers as you do so. Add some dry garden or kitchen waste as a further aid. Generally, the pile should be stirred weekly throughout the season.

Other hitches can occur on the way to making compost, but often these are odor-free. For example, leaves or grass clippings that are added during hot or dry weather in the summer or fall will decompose slowly because of a shortage of moisture. Adding water to the point that materials are moist to the touch will speed up decomposition.

Another common hitch occurs when too many carbon-containing materials are added, such as dry leaves in the autumn. This causes an imbalance in the carbon-nitrogen ratio. What's happened is that microbes have consumed the nitrogen in the pile and need a replenishment. The solution is to add nitrogen with grass clippings, kitchen scraps (but not meat products) or something similar.

It's not so much the smells or the apparent slowness of a pile that discourages people from composting, but the mystique that has been built around the whole issue. While it may be interesting to learn about psychrophiles, mesophiles and thermophiles, ambient temperature and its effect on activity of the microbes, the novice is best served by understanding the basics.

Perhaps the best place for practical help is a neighbor who you see frequently adding raw materials to a pile or bin and then harvesting finished compost weeks later. Cooperative extension offices often have helpful bulletins and the topic is usually covered in comprehensive gardening books.

Materials in compost bins will benefit from a thorough spring stirring before the growing and composting season gets underway. Shown demonstrating the proper stirring technique is the author's neighbor Jon Evans.

Leftover seeds and supplies may be okay

A garage is like a refrigerator in its capacity to hide leftovers that are stored with good intentions but are quickly forgotten.

Old fertilizer, unplanted bulbs, leftover seeds and half-empty bottles of weed killer are among the gardening things that can be unearthed in many garages this time of year. If one or more of these treasures are in your garage, and you are wondering what to do, here are some ideas:

- Unplanted tulips, daffodils and other bulbs – Throw 'em away. If they are not mushy and useless by now, they will be soon. Ditto for unplanted bulbs stored in the freezer under the assumption there is no difference between the cold in the freezer and the cold in the ground. There is a difference and the bulb knows it.

- Leftover seeds – Plant them when danger of frost has past. How many sprout depends on the type of seed and the climate inside your garage over winter. If you want to be sure your garden sprouts dependably this year, plant new seeds.

- Still-filled pots – The plants are likely dried out or mushy and are obviously useless. The soil may look fine but it's not. Container-bound soil degrades in a year or two. Better to work last year's soil back into the garden and buy fresh, made-for-container-gardening soil. Several manufacturers blend soil mixes specifically for container plantings and the label will say so.

- Old fertilizer – It's fine. Break up any lumps before pouring it in the spreader. Use a stick to do so as handling with bare hands can cause skin irritation.

- Unused garden chemicals – They are probably okay, although their potency may have diminished over winter.

Components of liquids can settle out of solution; a gentle shaking will reunite them. If you have concerns, call the manufacturer using the hotline number listed on the label. Many communities have a hazardous waste disposal day this time of year; dispose of unwanted chemicals this way.

The best way to avoid leftover chemicals is to buy only what's needed for the season, even if it means paying a higher price for the smaller container rather than the more economical jumbo size.

- Leftover gasoline – It's probably okay; if not, your mower or trimmer will run poorly. Poor running can also be the result of a bad spark plug, dirty air filter or ill-adjusted carburetor. Some gardeners preserve leftover gas over winter by adding a fuel stabilizing additive.

- Dirty pots – There may be unwanted disease and insect pests along with the caked-on dirt. Scrub with soap and water any pots you will reuse this year. Also, before planting a clay pot, submerge it in a pail of water so it will be saturated with moisture before it's planted.

Use fresh soil blended for containers each year for best results in windowbox and container plantings.

Little things early on pay off big later

The first few days transplants spend in the garden can spell success or trouble. Here's how to make it a success.

- Cold turkey – Homegrown transplants started on a windowsill or under lights are extremely tender. Help them make the transition from indoors to outdoors by first setting the plants outdoors during the day in a sheltered location. Exposure to cooler temperatures, wind and sun will toughen them. Five days of this treatment is sufficient.

  This process is called hardening off and some growers do this as a matter of course. But there is no way of telling by looking at the plants. Because of this, it is a good idea to give all annuals a few days transition time before planting.

- Warm soil – Most transplants cope better with cool air than with cool soil. Their roots will establish sooner if planted in warm soil. This is a key reason why it is better to set out transplants later in May than earlier. The other reason is chance of a killing frost diminishes with every passing day.

- Mini-greenhouses – Various protective caps and warming devices are available to protect plants set out early in the season. These keep the air and soil appreciably warmer in the area immediately around the plant and by doing so, can provide a two-week head start on the season. Folks who grow vegetables, especially tomatoes and peppers, really like these things because they bring summer vegetables to the table weeks earlier and give them bragging rights to the first ripe tomato of the season. Nothing wrong with that!

This tomato support system consists of wire cages and wooden supports. Many techniques are available and whichever is chosen, the important thing is to have it in place early in the season.

- Special fertilizers – My experience has been that fertilizers formulated to be applied when plants are first set out pay off. Plants seem to get off to a better start when given such a treatment.

- Cool roots – Impatiens and wax begonias are among bedding plants that do better throughout the season when the plants are mulched with shredded bark, wood chips or a similar material. The mulch keeps the soil evenly moist and, during the heat of the summer, cooler than surrounding soil. Take care not to heap mulch directly against the stems as this may lead to rotting.

- Supports – Put them in place early in the growing season and train plants accordingly. Those in particular need include tall varieties of snapdragons, cosmos and some dahlias and most varieties of tomatoes. Peonies are best supported as shoots emerge in mid-April. To protect from damaging winds and rain, use sturdier and bigger stakes than you think are needed.

Vigor in bedding plants counts more than pedigree

Supermarket or nursery? Farm market or home center? With bedding plants being sold everywhere, does it matter where you buy them?

Probably not.

What matters in terms of garden performance is the care the plants get from the time they leave the greenhouse until they are planted in your garden. Neglect along the way can cripple the plant for the season or simply slow it down for a few weeks.

Regardless of where you shop, here are some things to watch for when buying bedding plants:

- Evidence of care – Bedding plants need frequent watering because they are grown in a tiny mass of soil. Look for indications the store takes watering seriously. The presence of overhead sprinklers, hoses near the sales area or a sales associate continually tending the plants is a good sign.

- Evidence of freshness – Flats filled with sturdy and compact plants flush with bright, perky foliage are a sign the plants are fresh from the greenhouse. Plants that are store-weary show it: They lack luster, are lanky and often the roots are coming out of the bottom of the trays.

- Evidence of youth – Plants with no flowers or with more buds than blossoms are usually younger than those in full bloom in the flat. Young plants get off to a quicker start in the garden than older ones.

- Evidence of understanding – Flats of impatiens displayed in full sun suggests store personnel don't care or don't know that impatiens cannot tolerate hot sun unless mulched and watered frequently. Be wary of a store that displays its plants without regard to their need for sun or shade.

- Evidence of information – Hybridizing has led to lots of choices in any given type of plant in its size, foliage, color, flower time, disease resistance, fragrance and other variables. These variables are seldom apparent until midway through the season when it is too late to re-plant. Look for the plant tag in each tray to provide this important information.

- Evidence of help – While plant tags provide basic information, you may have questions about how your selection would look in a container, hanging basket, massed in a bed or similar treatments. You should expect this sort of help from a nursery and be willing to pay a little more money for it.

This tray of pansies was purchased at a discount store. It looks as good as one purchased from a nursery.

Now people (and birds) can enjoy sunflowers

Sunflowers have become so pretty and useful in recent years that you may not want to share their seedheads with the birds.

What a turnaround! Not many years ago, sunflowers came in one size: Huge. Many gardeners raised them either for the birds or to help youngsters with their first garden. While their teaching value was high, their overall garden value was low.

Today's sunflowers range in height from about 1 to 10 feet tall. The shortest ones are ideal for pots and the larger ones for screening or as a backdrop for shorter plants. Now, they are beautiful and versatile in the garden and as a source for cut flowers.

Some varieties bear blossoms in the classic sunflower color combo of gold petals and dark brown centers. Blooms of others move around the color wheel with petals in shades of mahogany, red, yellow, orange and cream. Some sport contrasting colors in the centers, others match the petal color.

Most varieties bear single blossoms but some have full, double blooms that resemble a dahlia. And to further add freedom of choice: Some bear one flower atop the central stem while others branch and produce flowers from side shoots freely all summer. Some don't have pollen and that's good because pollen can stain clothes and furniture.

Now's the time to plant sunflowers directly in the garden. They will sprout in 5 to 10 days and blossom 7 to 10 weeks later, depending on the variety. Some gardeners get a head start by starting seeds indoors in early May, but doing so is not necessary given the plant's rapid growth habit.

All sunflowers share a common need of a garden spot that gets full day sun and has rich, well-drained soil. Sphagnum peat moss or compost worked into a sandy or clay soil helps makes the soil more plant-friendly.

What variety to choose? Before grabbing the first packet from the seed rack, ask yourself these questions:

- Do I want it for screening? Choose a variety that grows at least six feet tall. Recommendation: 'Giant Sungold,' because of its height and 10-inch, double orange blooms.

- Do I want it for cut flowers? Choose a branching variety with repeat blooms and ideally, one that produces pollenless blossoms. Recommendation: 'Music Box' because of its height (28 inches), colors (yellow to mahogany) and prolific blooming.

- Do I want it for a container? Choose a dwarf variety that grows no more than 24 inches tall. Recommendation: 'Elf'; it grows about 16 inches tall and bears clear yellow blooms with yellow centers.

- Do I want it for bird seed? Choose a variety that grows tall and produces a huge head. Recommendation: 'Giganteus' or 'Russian Giant.'

Don't sweat if you can't find one of these varieties. With dozens of varieties in commerce, chances are excellent you'll find one that fits your needs perfectly. Look to the seed packet for details.

This sunflower grows 30 inches tall, making it an ideal background plant for shorter annuals. It is a branching variety so there'll be more flowers after the first ones fade.

Big deal in the garden ... surprise ... it's the color white

Your favorite flower color is ...?

Probably red, blue or yellow, according to a non-scientific survey I take each spring as bedding plants are popping up in stores everywhere. People say they like the red of geraniums, the blue of petunias and the yellow of marigolds. Seldom is a vote cast for white.

That's a shame because white is an extremely useful color in the garden, or as cut flowers, for these reasons:

- White reflects light. It is visible when the light is low, making it a perfect choice for shady areas or spots that will be viewed after dusk.

- White provides contrast. Other colors planted next to white stand out because of it, especially the deep pink and purple jewel tones popular in some varieties of geraniums and impatiens.

- That white is reflective and provides contrast is equally useful when choosing blossoms for an indoor bouquet. A few white blooms included in the bouquet make the others dazzle.

Spring is a great time to work white into your existing garden or plans for your summer garden. Here's where and what:

Cool season gardens – Pansies and violas are prolific bloomers when the temperature is below 75 degrees. They look best when planted in groups of 15 or more plants of the same type and color. Pansies bear larger flowers than violas, but the whites of both are equally dramatic. A nice touch is found in some of the pansy varieties that have white petals and a yellow throat.

Pansies and violas quit blooming when hot weather arrives. If kept watered and fertilized, they'll bloom nicely again in autumn and, often, the following spring.

Massed plantings – Choose among impatiens, wax begonias and petunias for a massed planting. Each grows stocky with lots of side shoots and flowers. Petunias tend to be the tallest of the trio, followed by impatiens and then wax begonias. Petunias have the largest flowers, wax begonias the smallest.

Wax begonias and impatiens require no maintenance while petunias do best if dead flowers are continually removed and the plant sheared in late summer to re-energize it. Petunias need full sun. Wax begonias do fine in partial shade or sunny areas, but will balk if planted where they get hot afternoon sun for hours on end. Impatiens do better in partial shade but some varieties are equally at home in sunny areas. Actually, most impatiens will do fine in full sun providing their roots are kept cool and moist. This is easily done by spreading a two-inch blanket of wood chips, shredded bark or similar organic mulch around the base of the plants.

Ground cover plantings – While perennials are usually the choice for ground cover, annuals such as alyssum and portulaca (moss rose) make ideal ground covers for one season. White alyssum is especially nice when planted as a ground cover in a bed of geraniums. There's something about the zillions of small white flowers that contrast nicely with the foliage and flowers of geraniums. Some varieties of alyssum are fragrant.

Portulaca is mostly sold as mixes of several colors, rather than pure white. Portulaca likes it hot and sunny. Alyssum can deal with full sun or light shade.

Background plantings – In the back of the garden and to provide tall cut flowers, it's hard to beat white snapdragons, zinnias and dahlias. White marigolds aren't very white, compared to these other choices, however. There are a few varieties of white roses but, in my opinion, they tend to be weak bushes and stingy bloomers.

Trellis and fence plantings – The morning glory and moon flower are great for a mass of white blossoms, especially if planted in a sunny and hot area with poor to mediocre soil. The individual morning glory blossom lasts only one day; still, if you pick a cluster of buds, you can enjoy fresh morning glory flowers indoors for several days.

For perennials, clematis would be my choice. This plant takes several years to get established but once it's happy, it's a prolific bloomer. White clematis would be a great choice against a background of dark brick or siding.

White flowers from bulbs, perennials and annuals brighten dark areas of the landscape and provide color in the evening after the sun sets.

How to fix good things that turn bad in the yard

Good things have a way of turning bad over time in a landscape.

A tree support cuts a groove into the bark. A ground cover planting invades the yard, choking out good grass. The vigor of a rosebush ebbs away. Here's how to deal with these and other good-turns-bad situations:

- Tree support – Check the band around the trunk every six months and ease or tighten the tension so the band is taunt with anchoring wires attached to stakes in the ground. Better to err on the loose side, because a too-tight fit will cut into the trunk as it grows outward.

The deep cut in the trunk of this Norway maple is the result of a tree band left in place too long. Shown is the author's brother, Mike Hutchison.

- Invading groundcovers – Given a chance, lily-of-the-valley, ivy, myrtle and similar ground covers will spread into the lawn. Once there, they are difficult to eradicate because they resist herbicides and their roots defy complete removal.

Keep 'em in bounds with a six-inch-deep strip of edging between the lawn and groundcover bed. Or, maintain a deep, natural edge between the areas and every few months, cut through it with a shovel to sever whatever roots are inching outward.

- Roses go bad – Most modern roses are two bushes in one. The named (grafted) variety and root stock. Sometimes canes grow up from the root stock and, if left unattended, choke the vigor of the named variety, especially when it's weak. Cut off the suckers when you first see them.

Maintaining the named variety's health is the best way to keep the root stock from trying to assume control. Feed the bush monthly during the growing season and check frequently for signs of insect or disease. I prefer to use systemic insecticide to control insects as this material provides protection for several weeks and fungicides to control diseases. As with any garden chemical, read and follow label instructions.

- Grass gives up – Grass that sprouts in the spring only to die in the summer is a sign the area may be too shady to support season-long growth. When trees leaf out to form a dense canopy, the spring-green grass is in trouble.

Solution: Sow fresh grass seed that is shade tolerant and remove tree limbs to a height of 10 feet so more light is available to the grass. Grass will not grow in dense shade so eventually you may have to give up and leave the ground bare, spread mulch or try a shade-tolerant groundcover.

- Flowering shrubs don't bloom – Not enough full sun is a key reason why lilacs, forsythia and other flowering shrubs won't bloom but otherwise seem healthy. As a landscape matures, trees grow and throw shade that deepens over the years. A once prolific bloomer gradually becomes a non-bloomer. Solution: Move the bush to a sunny area. Also, prune out old branches to the ground and feed every year. Fertilizer spikes are an easy and practical way to do so.

- Perennials grow poorly – Most perennials should be divided every three to five years, especially those that grow quickly. Doing so re-energizes the plant. Daylilies, hosta, ornamental grasses, rudbeckia and astilbe are a few of the popular perennials that benefit from this treatment. Lift the roots carefully from the soil and split the root mass into three or more divisions. Discard any portion that seems to be dead or diseased. Replant the divisions and water in. This task is usually best done in the autumn, about the time plants lose their leaves.

Garden not in yet? It's not too late

Don't give up on a garden this year if lack of time, energy or good weather has prevented you from considering one until now. If you act soon, you'll find plenty of plants and growing time to have a splendid garden.

Not many years ago, the supply of bedding plants pretty much dried up by Memorial Day because most folks had their gardens in by then. Now, growers bring on fresh crops of flowers and vegetables to be garden-ready as late as early July.

Starting a garden now is a bit different than putting one in at the usual time in mid-May. Here are some tips to help you succeed with what the traditional gardener's calendar would say is a late start:

- Seeds or transplants? – While most vegetable and flower seeds sprout in just 7 to 14 days, eight or more weeks are needed to reach flowering or fruiting maturity. This is true of impatiens, petunias, alyssum, pansies, tomatoes and peppers, to name a few. Better to make up for lost time by setting out transplants, rather than sowing seeds. When shopping, choose young, stocky plants rather than tall ones in flower.

There's no problem in planting seeds of quick growers like marigolds, zinnias, sunflowers, lettuce, radishes and cucumbers. Check the seed packet to learn when the plant will bear fruit or flowers and choose the variety that takes the least time, providing its other attributes are to your liking.

- Jump start feeding – When plants are in or seeds have sprouted, treat the youngsters to a weak solution of fertilizer. In normal seasons, this task can wait until several weeks after planting; doing so now will help the plant establish itself more quickly and step right into the heart of the summer. Some brands of fertilizers are formulated especially for this early feeding. After the initial start-up fertilizer, feed every month or so.

Regardless of when your garden is started, take care not to over fertilize as doing so will force the plant to grow leaves at the expense of blossoms. You want a steady supply of buds if you are growing vegetables or flowers.

- Mulch helps – A blanket of mulch keeps the soil moist and temperatures constant, factors that help plants settle in quickly. Impatiens and wax begonias, especially, benefit from a protective mulch. Shredded bark or chips work great; avoid grass clippings because they mat and block the free flow of water and air and may have leftover weed killer that could kill the plants.

■ Water smartly – Roots of newly planted transplants and seedlings don't reach very far yet for water, so take care to keep the new plants watered sufficiently. Sufficient means they won't wilt, even under stress of wind and hot temperatures. Letting a plant wilt only to revive it with water wastes growing time and the plant's energy.

■ Deadheading – Removing spent blossoms is called deadheading and it is a worthwhile practice for zinnias, marigolds, geraniums, snapdragons and other annuals with large or many-petalled blossoms. Some annuals, such as wax begonias, impatiens, alyssum and others with small flowers drop wilted blooms automatically.

But those that don't drop blooms automatically will begin setting seed as the flower wilts and this takes energy that could otherwise go to more flower production. Keep dead flowers picked off to keep the plant blooming all summer long, with nary a day devoted to seed production.

A blanket of shredded bark helps get these white petunias off to a quick start. Mulch moderates soil temperatures, conserves soil moisture and keeps weeds in check.

Disbudding and feeding leads to big blooms

You can coax big flowers from peonies, roses, zinnias and other plants by practicing a technique called disbudding.

Disbudding consists of removing side buds from a stem so the plant's energy goes into growing just one flower, not several.

Commercial growers practice disbudding to produce big roses, carnations and similar florist crops. Home gardeners don't seem to be aware of it.

Side buds are best removed when they are tiny. That's because they are easiest to remove then and leave little trace as the main flower develops. Rolling the bud between a thumb and forefinger removes it easily.

Disbudding is most practical on plants that produce a strong, central bud. Hybrid tea roses, peonies and tall varieties of zinnias and carnations are the major ones. Disbudding is not a good idea for floribunda roses because their flowers look best when clustered. Nor is it needed for annuals like impatiens, petunias, verbena, celosia and most others that are grown for a massed flower effect.

Another way to keep big flowers coming is to be diligent in removing spent blossoms and keeping the plant well fed. This is especially important now, early in the season, as plants are beginning their first strong bloom cycle.

Impatiens, wax begonias, alyssum and most annuals with small flowers drop wilted blooms cleanly and automatically. Some that should be removed include geraniums, zinnias, marigolds, calendula, celosia, snapdragons, salvia, dahlias and tuberous begonias.

Removing spent blossoms encourages the plant to put out new growth, rather than producing seed.

Regular feeding is also important to keep plants in bloom. Geraniums and roses are big feeders and do best when fed monthly. Some annuals thrive in poor soil and want little fertilizer; check the tag that came with your annuals to be sure.

While overfeeding can result in the plant producing more leaves than flowers, it is a relatively slight risk. I garden in Michigan where the season is short so I keep the plants producing blossoms with monthly feedings. I use granular fertilizer for roses and water-soluble fertilizer for annuals and perennials.

If too much fertilizer is used, the plant will signal this condition by producing a lot of leaves at the expense of flower buds. When this happens, simply reduce the frequency of feeding.

Really big flowers like these peony blossoms result from removing side buds and feeding plants regularly.

Slow decomposition to stretch life of mulch

June is mulch month in most parts of the country.

It's either get it down now or waste the benefits it provides as summer moves forward. Among the benefits: Reduced weeding and watering since mulch conserves soil moisture and chokes weeds. This means less work in the yard and more time to do more enjoyable things.

Maintaining a mulched garden or big areas around the perimeter of the house carries with it a stiff price. Mulch is expensive, time consuming to put down and usually has to be renewed every other year because it breaks down rapidly.

With a few exceptions, I am not a mulch fan for those reasons. The exceptions: Beds that cannot be watered regularly because of extended vacation or travel and plantings that benefit greatly from a blanket of mulch. Impatiens, for example, can be grown in full sun providing the soil is kept cool and moist, and mulch helps to do so.

If you mulch, do so smartly. Here's how:

- If practical, install an underlayment of landscape fabric. This is cloth-like stuff that lets water and air through the layer of mulch. My experience has been that landscape fabric adds another year to the useful life of mulch by slowing down its decomposition. This is probably because it reduces its contact with soil microbes that break down organic materials, like mulch.

Some gardeners use black plastic sheeting or discarded plastic garment bags as an underlayment. I am not in favor of these materials because they do not let air and moisture pass freely between soil and mulch. This could set up an unhealthy growing environment for plants in the area.

Underlayment is a pain to install because of the cutting and fitting involved. The effort is most practical in areas where there won't be any changes in the plantings, like around the house. If there's going to be a lot of digging in the area, don't bother with it.

- Use materials that break down slower than others. I've found that shredded cypress bark and hardwood chips last about one year longer than shredded bark. Hardwood nuggets seem to last even longer. Pea gravel or larger stones last essentially forever. Before using a rock mulch, be sure it's what you really want because it is more expensive, heavy to move and difficult to remove should you change your mind.

- Install a chemical weed barrier underneath the mulch. Products such as "Preen" keep weed seeds from sprouting for about a year. They are sprinkled on the soil, raked and watered in. They are easy and inexpensive to apply. Weed seeds that lodge in the mulch above the material, though, will sprout. As with any garden chemical, please read and heed label instructions.

A landscape fabric under mulch in areas where there will be little additional planting, such as in this bed, will lengthen the life of the mulch.

Plants won't go thirsty if a few conditions are met

Garden and landscape plants don't have to go thirsty this or any summer – regardless of how hot and dry it gets outdoors. Nor do you have to spend every waking moment watering.

Providing the moisture plants need doesn't take much work, water or money. Instead, abundant moisture is the cumulative result of several small gardening practices. With spring slipping into summer, now is a good time to review a few of these measures.

- If water is needed, apply it in the morning so the plant is better able to withstand afternoon heat without wilting. Evening watering is not a good idea because it sets up conditions that prompt harmful disease.

- Water the ground around the plant with soaker hoses or drip irrigation devices. Sprinklers and nozzles are wasteful because much of the water is blown away or lands where it is not efficiently used by the plant. Also, disease is spread by water splashing from overhead watering, especially among roses, zinnias and some vegetables.

- Add sphagnum peat moss (the stuff that's dry and comes in plastic bales) to the soil, especially when planting new trees and shrubs. The moss is like a sponge and helps keep moisture and nutrients near the plant's roots, where they are most needed.

- Cover the soil in the garden area with a two- to five- inch layer of mulch. Mulch is helpful because it holds in moisture and keeps the soil cool. Partially decomposed materials like compost, wood chips, shredded bark and well-rotted manure are the best. The only real drawback with mulch is that it usually needs replenishing every year and that means time and money.

Landscape fabric is a good second choice because it is inexpensive and also porous, which lets air and moisture pass through. Grass clippings are okay, but only as a last resort because they tend to mat down and may become so dense that water can't get through to the ground. Don't use clippings if weed killer has been applied within the past six weeks.

- Whenever possible, group plants with similar water needs together. Generally, plants with a lot of leaves or very large leaves are high water users because of moisture lost through the accumulated leaf area. Established trees fall in this class and their roots can usually find enough moisture. However, even they may need supplemental water during prolonged dry spells.

- Be sure there's ample moisture during key times in a plant's life cycle. This is especially important in the vegetable garden between the time blossoms appear and fruit is set.

- Be mindful that rain seldom reaches plantings under overhangs and that supplemental water is usually needed every week or so, even in times of abundant rainfall. This situation is compounded by the fact that the soil around a home's foundation is often sandy and doesn't hold moisture well.

- Plants in containers should be checked at least daily to be sure the soil is moist. Water evaporates quickest from clay pots, but even plastic pots bear watching because of the swift drying effects of sun and wind.

Gentle breezes – the kind that dry clothes on the line so nicely – are tough on leafy plants. On breezy days, check the garden to see if it is drying out quicker than normal.

- Recognize the signs of distress. Leaves and stems will first wilt and appear lifeless and if dryness continues, they will collapse. A plant can usually be revived without lasting damage if it has only wilted. If its stems collapse, then lasting damage has been done and it may not recover.

Much of the sphagnum peat moss used by American gardeners to improve garden soil comes from Canada. Here, a harvester has just vacuumed and gathered peat loosened from the bog by another machine. Next, the peat will be cleaned and bagged.

Try bougainvillea and hibiscus for a tropical look

Hot and sunny summer months offer gardeners a chance to enjoy flowers of the tropics at home, even though their climate includes snow and cold over winter.

Bougainvillea and hibiscus are the plants of choice because of their unusual flower color, shape and size. Bougainvillea bears great clusters of blossoms in vibrant, clear red, pink, yellow, copper and white. Red and pink are the most common. Leaves are glossy light green and the plant has growth characteristics of a vine.

Hibiscus blossoms are a whopping 5 inches across; some varieties approach 12 inches. Red, apricot and white are the most prevalent colors with red being the easiest to find. With most varieties, each flower lasts but one day, opening in the morning and wilting at dusk. A healthy plant is seldom without flower, though. Foliage is dark green, resembling an elm leaf, and the plant has a bushy appearance.

Both crave heat and at least half-day sun. Days should be at least 70 and nights no cooler than 60. While this seems like an easy-enough growing mix to provide, it is a little tricky.

The secret to a continual parade of flowers is in providing consistently warm evening temperatures, especially in late summer.

I've had good luck growing both by treating them as big houseplants, potted in large containers filled with soil blended for houseplants. I set the pots on the deck, which gets lots of bright sun from 11 a.m. to 5 p.m. The heat of the late afternoon sun is softened by shade cast from nearby oak and maple trees. There is some retained warmth from the house that keeps the plants a few degrees warmer at night than if they were out in the yard. The deck area is a microclimate that's sunnier and warmer than most other areas of the yard.

If you measure the quality of the summer by the number of hot and sunny days, either hibiscus or bougainvillea will be an accurate indicator. Cool, cloudy spells slow down flowering and overall growth of the plant. Likewise, a run of hot, sunny weather has these plants popping blooms like firecrackers. They are fun to watch in this regard.

Other than sun and warmth, neither is fussy. They do best when fed monthly with the same fertilizer used for annuals. Their watering needs do differ, however. Hibiscus is best when the soil is continually moist. Soil for bougainvillea should be allowed to dry out slightly between waterings.

Both can be wintered over indoors, provided there's a spot indoors that gets a lot of sun. Without sufficient sun indoors, the plant will slow down growth and flowering. It will kick back in high gear when put outdoors in the summer. At that point, trim back leggy portions of the plant to force out new growth. After a summer of robust growth, it may be necessary to repot. If so, use fresh houseplant soil and a slightly larger container with drainage.

A native of Brazil, bougainvillea is an excellent pot plant to enjoy during the summer. The light-colored wall behind this specimen reflects helpful heat back to the plant.

Lawns dry out quickly now, but you can help

A run of hot and dry days in early summer demonstrates how quickly an unwatered lawn can lose its lush, green glow.

The situation seems to occur once every few years. Moist and cool weather in late spring keeps lawns green and growing so there is no hurry to start up the irrigation system or find the sprinkler amid the piles of stuff in the garage.

Then hot weather hits. The lawn isn't watered and sure enough, it dries out quickly. Several days of watering, or rain, are needed to restore its spring glow. If you want to keep your lawn lush this summer, here's how to handle watering:

- Water early in the day so the grass is hydrated to face the heat of the day. Finish up by noon.

- If there's no rain and you must depend on a hose and sprinkler, water twice a week, leaving the sprinkler in place 30 minutes.

- If you have an irrigation system, find a cycle that best fits your yard. A basic schedule might consist of 20-minute cycles for each zone every other day, plus a 10-minute mid-afternoon spritz for zones in full sun. Turn the system off during rainy periods, unless you have a dependable rain sensor that automatically cancels scheduled cycles during rainy periods.

- Watch for off-colored areas as these are a sign that water is not reaching that spot. Footprints that don't bounce back are also a sign the grass is thirsty. Dry spots like these often crop up at the far reaches of a sprinkler, especially oscillating types.

  Another dry-spot culprit: Irrigation systems that have not been adjusted recently to allow for trees and shrubs that have grown to block the water stream. Use a rain gauge, coffee tin or similar container to get a rough measure of how much water is being applied. The general guideline is that a lawn needs one inch of water each week, be it from irrigation or rain.

- Most of all, maintain whatever watering schedule helps your yard keep its spring green glow. The times mentioned in this article are meant to be examples only. The best timing for your yard depends on varying conditions, such as soil type, type of grasses, health of lawn and exposure to sun.

Other things to keep your lawn green, growing and happy all summer: Feed it at least once during the summer and have the lawnmower blade professionally sharpened so it cuts, rather than tears at, grass. Mulching mowers, especially, require a sharp blade to chop up grass in small pieces.

A quick adjustment to a sprinkler head is often all that's needed to get the right amount of water to a lawn that is drying out in spots.

Cut flowers last days longer with proper care

Summer flowers are plentiful now, both from the garden and farm markets. How they are prepared for "vase life" makes a big difference in how good they look and for how long.

Here are some tips to consider.

Before cutting – Choose buds that show color and are beginning to unfurl. If a bud appears to be too tight, it probably is. Give it another day before harvesting.

Early morning and early evening are the best times of day to cut as this is when sugar and moisture levels are highest and ample supplies of both help to prolong blossom life.

A sharp knife provides the cleanest cut, especially for woody plants like roses. A pair of scissors is fine for zinnias, marigolds and similar annuals.

During cutting – Cut no more of a stem than is needed and at a point that encourages new growth to break out. This is just above the first set of five leaves on a rose and usually at a similar junction of stem and side branches of annuals.

Immediately after cutting, strip off a few sets of lower leaves from each stem and plunge the stem into the pail of water you have carried to the garden. If the stem is not in water immediately, the end quickly dries out, sealing itself and shortening the blossom's life. Some wilted blooms will bounce back when re-cut and put in water, others won't.

After cutting – If time permits, give the pail of blossoms a few hours rest in a cool, airy spot before arranging. Doing so gives the blooms a chance to draw up moisture before being subjected to the rigors of arranging and display. This also gives you time to choose a vase that meets your decorating needs and that of the flowers. For the flowers' sake, choose a vase that holds plenty of water and is big enough to accommodate stems and blossoms without cramming.

Florist foam ("Oasis" is one brand) works well as a means of holding flowers in place for fancy arrangements. The foam must be saturated with water before using and secured in the container to prevent the arrangement from toppling. Only the stem and not the leaves should be inserted into the foam and once inserted, should not be moved.

If it's necessary to re-position the stem, insert it elsewhere in the foam as the original hole will fill with air that will seal off the stem from its water supply. Chicken wire, glass marbles and similar devices also help hold flowers in place.

Fresh water is your best ally in keeping blossoms fresh. Change it daily if possible, rinsing off the end of the stems at the same time. This keeps bacterial growth down and by doing so, prolongs the life of the blossom. Fresh flower preservative powder is helpful, especially if the arrangement is such that water can't be changed daily.

My understanding is these materials retard bacterial growth in the water. Over the years, I've added pennies and aspirin to the water, as some consider these good preservatives. On balance, I don't think they do much good. I prefer to change water daily because, in my opinion, fresh water is the best preservative of them all.

To enjoy the longest life from cut flowers, harvest blossoms as buds are beginning to unfurl. While beautiful, this rose blossom is about one day beyond its prime "cut time."

Remove obstacles to make mowing go quicker

You can reduce the time it takes to mow your lawn by getting rid of obstacles that interfere with a speedy but thorough job.

Here's a review of common obstacles that are often overlooked, and what can be done to eliminate them. Eliminating means investing time and effort up front, but the payback is in mowing the yard in less time, and still doing a good job.

Obstacle #1 – Trees and the need to trim grass that grows around them.

Solution #1 – Install a ring of mulch or ground cover around each tree to eliminate the need to trim at the trunk. Use plastic edging to define the ring and keep grass from growing inside. A large ring usually looks better than a smaller one, so err on the side of a big circle.

A ring of mulch around a tree saves mowing time by eliminating the need to trim around the trunk.

Obstacle #2 – Tree or shrub branches that cause you to duck or swerve to avoid being poked.

Solution #2 – Prune off low branches back to the trunk and at a height that lets you walk under the tree without being assaulted. Low branches of young trees are seldom an obstacle while mowing, although selectively pruning back while young will force out top growth. This solution is good for the tree and the grass or ground cover underneath as it allows more sun, air and water to reach the ground below the tree's canopy.

Obstacle #3 – Grass grows around fence posts and the fence line and beyond the mower's reach.

Solution #3 – Create a narrow no-grass zone along the length of the fence. This means putting in heavy-duty plastic edging along both sides of the fence and filling the area between with mulch. Installing such a zone is a pain, but once it's done, you'll be able to mow up to the edging and not have to worry about grass growing beyond the mower's reach.

Obstacle #4 – Gardens and plantings around the house are arranged in a way that requires a lot of short, inefficient swipes to cut the grass between the area and lawn.

Solution #4 – Next time you lay out a planting, do so in a way that lets you mow in an efficient, continuous run. Straight lines are okay, but long and gentle curves are more attractive.

Existing beds can be easily modified by adding gentle curves to straight runs or runs with sharp curves that require a lot of twisting of the mower to navigate. Add heavy-duty plastic edging to keep grass from growing in the bed.

Obstacle #5 – Mail box and lamp posts, strips along the deck or patio, air conditioners and the barbecue grill and similar human-made obstacles require extra chunks of time to keep tidy.

Solution #5 – Look for ways to eliminate grass from obstacles. Your most dependable allies will usually be heavy-duty plastic edging to create a no-grass zone and a filler material (stones, shredded bark, ground cover) to keep grass from invading the area and taking your time to trim.

Choose trees carefully to achieve years of beauty

If homeowners practiced the same good sense exemplified by a Southerner 300 years ago, there would be fewer overgrown trees and shrubs banging against the house and crowding out the natural shape of each other.

What the Southerner did was choose the right plant and put it in the right place to create a dramatic entrance for a mansion that would one day overlook the Mississippi River in Vacherie, La.

Dramatic it is. Two rows, each with 14 Live Oak trees (Quercus virginiana), stretch one-quarter mile to the entrance of the mansion that was built in 1837, long after the oaks had been planted. Known as Oak Alley Plantation, it has been the setting for countless films. Fans of the soap "Days of Our Lives" may recognize it as the spot where characters Hope Williams and Beau Brady honeymooned.

The canopy of each tree reaches 100 feet across, just touching its neighbor planted 80 feet away. Each tree was spaced so at maturity, it would have room on the ground and in the air. Collectively, they create a massive promenade leading to the home. This type of oak is said to have a potential life expectancy of 600 years. That means they may be alive hundreds of years beyond the millennium.

Hundreds of year old, this stately planting of Live Oak trees welcomes visitors to the Oak Alley Plantation in Vacherie, La.

With summer in full swing and lots of nursery stock ready for immediate planting, now is a good time to consider the lesson of Oak Alley.

The Southern planter chose a tree that would prosper in the deep South. He picked one that would grow very old and do so gracefully. He planted each far enough apart to complement, rather than compete with, each other. You can make the same decisions and choices for your home, and by doing so, replicate the success of Oak Alley in your landscaping.

First of all, make sure the tree is suitable for your growing area. Your nurseryman can help, or if shopping by catalog, pay attention to details about the plant's growing zone. There probably is a zone map in the catalog and this will help you make a good match.

Avoid trees that are short-lived or not desirable, such as European white birch (Betula pendula) and Eastern cottonwood, or Eastern poplar (Populus deltoides). Inexpensive to buy and easy to grow, they are not good choices for a lasting landscape because they die young and are messy to clean up after, given their propensity to drop weak branches and twigs.

Think twice about trees that age poorly. For example, the Colorado blue spruce (Picea pungens) is enormously popular because of the silvery-blue color of its needles and Christmas tree shape. But as it ages, branches sag and the classic shape so prominent and desirable in its youth disappears.

You would do well to steer clear of trees that can be a maintenance nuisance on the city lot. The white or weeping willow (Salix alba) comes to mind. It is a horrible tree, in my opinion, because of its weak branches, late dropping leaves and roots that seem to make a beeline for the nearest drain tile, septic field or sewer drain. Not anywhere as bad, but still troublesome, is the Norway maple (Acer platanoides). It is troublesome because its roots rise to the surface of the soil over time, making it hard to mow underneath.

Even a desirable tree and shrub will become problematic if planted too close to others or to a building. Trees with fine manners can quickly grow to become little more than a mass of shapeless green that no amount of pruning can remedy.

I made a big mistake on two counts when we landscaped our new home: I chose a European white birch and then planted it in a tight alcove between the garage and house. It looked fine for a few years but the branches soon grew to reach the second story and on windy days, scraped against the siding. At night, that's a spooky sound.

Like other European white birch, it fell prey to the ravishes of bronze birch border and leaf miner. I kept both somewhat under control with systemic insecticide, but after eight years of effort, the tree finally looked more dead than alive and it was removed. What's unfortunate is not that a tree fell to the axe, but the eight years invested in growing the tree would have been better used with a different tree that would have grown to fit the space available and not be so troubled by insects.

What we can all do is learn from and emulate the success at Oak Alley: Choose a tree and shrub knowing full well how big it gets, how quickly it gets there and any peculiarities it will encounter along the way. Do your homework before shopping and ask the nurseryman a lot of questions if you are not sure.

Your vacation can be tough on plants back home

Your summer vacation can be as stressful to the lawn and plants you leave behind as it is to your savings account.

Fortunately, it's easier to make amends to green growing things than to bankers. Here are some ideas to help you prevent plant problems while you're gone or fix ones on your return.

Container plants – Plants in containers often wilt if deprived of water for more than three days. A water-conserving soil mix can help, but that must be used when the container is made up.

In my experience fuchsia, strawflower and bacopa are especially sensitive to dry spells and seldom recover completely once they wilt to the point of drooping. Bacopa is relatively new on the container scene. It has small leaves and when flourishing, is covered with tiny white flowers. Most other plants used in containers will respond to water.

First-aid consists of submerging the wilted basket in a tub of warm water until bubbles stop rising to the surface. Place it in a shady spot and prune off whatever branches don't spring back. Feed the plants with a half-strength solution of liquid plant food and return them to their original home after several days rest in the shade.

Joy Hutchison uses an old-fashioned wash basin filled with water to start the revival process of a container plant that got a bit on the dry side.

For future absences, fill the top of the basket with shredded bark or a similar organic mulch. If the container is normally kept in a sunny, exposed area, move it to a shadier area for a few days. The lack of sun will cause it less harm than losing moisture quickly in sunny spots.

Garden flowers and vegetables – By this time of summer, plants are well-established in the garden and typically can survive 7 to 10 days without water. The key word is survive, not thrive. They cope by slowing down production of leaves and flowers. Some vegetables won't set fruit, even though blossoms are present and have been pollinated.

Your best response is to slowly restore moisture to the soil with a soaker hose stretched out close to the plants. A bubbler or similar soil-soaking device works well, too. Give the entire area a good soaking one day and another a few days later. The idea is to drive moisture into the soil 6 to 10 inches deep.

Next time for the garden? As with container plants, a layer of organic mulch over the surface greatly reduces moisture loss and helps the plants thrive in your absence.

The lawn – Grass goes dormant this time of year if there's not enough water. This is a protective mechanism that is both good and bad. The good is that much of the grass plant is very much alive and will green up later in the summer when rainfall and cooler weather return. The bad is that because the grass stops growing, weeds can quickly move in. This is how crabgrass gets such a hold this time of year. It thrives in the hot, dry weather that is misery for good grasses.

If your lawn has turned brown over vacation and it is your intention to green it back up again, then simply run the sprinkler every third day or so. Generally, a lawn needs an inch of water each week to stay green and growing. It will take a week or two before the lawn shows much sign of greening up.

If a brown lawn doesn't bother you, then leave it alone. Chances are excellent it will begin greening up in mid-August and will be growing vigorously again by mid-September. Watch for crabgrass, and get rid of it as soon as it's spotted. Wait until September, though, to eradicate dandelions and other broadleaf weeds. They are growing rapidly then and herbicides will be most effective.

For next summer, prepare your lawn for vacation by gradually cutting back on water beginning three weeks before your departure. This will condition grass plants to get used to progressively less water. A lawn conditioned in this manner is likely to green up more quickly when normal watering habits are restored after vacation.

It's also a good idea to mow high (three to three and one-half inches) throughout the lawn mowing season. Tall grass blades helpfully shade the crown of the plant.

Headaches and joys prevail in the August garden

To a plant, the lazy, hazy, crazy days of summer can be either a tonic or trouble.

Portulaca, salvia, marigold, gazania and morning glories are among annual flowers that soak up the heat with pleasure. Conversely, dianthus and pansies prefer much cooler weather and often quit blooming until things cool down. Snapdragons are iffy at summer's peak.

Heat and humidity are two factors the gardener can't control. Here's a snapshot look at other summer conditions that the gardener can do something about.

Mid-summer blahs – Some types of petunias grow leggy as summer progresses. The grandiflora (big bloom) varieties of petunias are especially prone to leggy and lethargic habits at mid-summer. The cure: Trim the plants to a height of six inches and fertilize. This will force new growth and within a few weeks, the plants will once again be covered with flowers.

I'm impressed with a new variety of petunia called 'Purple Wave.' It is colorful, seems to thrive on summer heat and is not disturbed by heavy rains. Flowers are a bright purple and on the smallish side. It gets about eight inches high and spreads to form a thick carpet of bright flowers and attractive foliage. If you like petunias but not their summer manners, try 'Purple Wave' or another of the 'Wave' varieties.

Pest and pestilence – Mites and aphids multiply rapidly during hot, humid weather and are a constant threat to plants putting out the new, tender growth these insects prefer. Roses are especially susceptible to mites although most annuals get them too. These and other insects are best controlled with a systemic insecticide that protects for up to six weeks because it stays in the plant's sap and is not washed away by rain.

Michigan horticulturist Chuck Martin recommends roses be treated to an occasional overhead watering. In his garden, he uses an ordinary oscillating sprinkler to do so. The falling water flushes away grime, which can interfere with photosynthesis, from the leaves. Overhead watering is best done at mid-day so there is plenty of strong light and air movement to help the leaves dry quickly.

Some annuals are struck by a number of diseases. Asters are especially prone to rust and zinnias to powdery mildew. My experience has been that disease problems with zinnias can be minimized with routine applications of fungicide but that diseased aster plants are best removed from the garden and destroyed. As with any garden chemical, please read and heed label instructions.

Crabgrass – This invasive annual grass ranks as the summer's number-one headache. It grows gloriously during the heat of the summer and within a few weeks of sprouting, begins to crowd out good grasses and soon dominates a dinner plate-sized area that once was turf. The trick is to eradicate the plant before it sends out seeds.

Do your lawn and your neighbors' a huge favor by eradicating crabgrass as soon as it's seen. Because it's an annual, it can be destroyed by pulling from the ground, although it's more effective to get rid of it with crabgrass killer. This is best done in the spring with a pre-emergent herbicide, followed with a post-emergent product if needed.

Marigolds and salvia are among annuals that bask in summer heat.

Fruit trees bear best when pollination needs are met

When fruit trees don't bear fruit, the cause is often attributed to the shortage of bees available for pollination.

I'm not a bee expert and I've read that the use of pesticides and urbanization has reduced the bee population, so maybe there are fewer bees available. My guess is that the real culprit for fruitless trees and shrubs is the gardener's lack of knowledge of what's required for a fruit or ornamental plant to bear productively.

Bees, and the wind, are vital to fruit setting on many plants because pollen must be transferred from one blossom to another before fruit can begin growing.

Most fruits require the pollen from the male part of a flower to be transferred to the female parts of a flower. The pollen must be of the right type, too. For example, apple pollen will not pollinate a pear blossom. In fact, it may not pollinate an apple blossom of another variety.

Flowers on self-fertile or self-pollinating plants can be fertilized by pollen from either flowers on the same plant or another of the same kind and, in the case of self-fertile plants, even if the "host" plant is some distance away. Examples of self-fertile plants include some apples, most peaches, all sour cherries, crabapples and strawberries.

Self-sterile plants will set fruit only with pollen from a plant of a different variety. Examples include many apples, all sweet cherries and some pears, peaches, apricots and plums. These plants need a pollinator within 100 feet and one that blooms at about the same time.

Some plants have male and female flowers on separate plants. Ornamental holly is one example. For berries to be set, there must be both male and female plants reasonably close together. Variety names tell the difference – 'Blue Boy' and 'Blue Girl,' 'Prince' and 'Princess,' for example.

Confusing? Sure is, because there are no 100 percent firm rules. It's important to ask questions of the nurseryman or read the catalog description carefully before buying a fruit-setting plant to be sure its pollination requirements can be met by plants you have or can add.

Back to the bees. They are instrumental in making pollination happen effectively and that usually means within a few hours or at most, days, after the blossom has opened.

Plants differ in the pollen and nectar that is produced and naturally, if bees are going to fly a mile in search of these supplies, they'll favor the plants that produce the most. Here's a partial listing of plants that bees favor for this reason.

Perennials – Achillea, baby's breath, bleeding heart, candytuft, coral bells, coreopsis, dahlia, geum, hollyhock, hydrangea, sedum and violet.

Annuals – Alyssum, balsam, calendula, celosia, cosmos, marigold, morning glory, salvia, sunflower and zinnia.

Herbs – Basil, chives, lavender, peppermint, rosemary and thyme.

Vegetables – Beans, corn, cucumber, lima bean, melons, peas, pepper, pumpkin, squash and watermelon.

What's convenient is that most of these are flowers and vegetables that people like growing because they are easily grown and produce a lot of flowers or vegetables. Add in the bonus that bees favor them, too, and that will go a long way in keeping a backyard orchard bountiful.

Understanding the pollination requirements of apples is vital to success. Shown with a dwarf tree in his Michigan orchard is Charles R. Baker.

Like puppies, cute trees grow big – too big, sometimes

It might be a good idea if shrubs and trees at the nursery carried a label that read: "WARNING – this plant will grow."

Perhaps such a label would encourage us to first learn if the tree or shrub will fit the space allocated for it when it reaches mature size.

Indeed, that cute Colorado blue spruce tree that's now just 18 inches tall has the genetic potential to grow 40 feet tall in 25 years. Is this a tree you want five feet from your front door?

With the fall planting season here, now is a good time to review the basics, the most basic of which is to plan for the future when choosing trees and shrubs.

I'm as guilty of ignoring the basics as the next guy, having just ripped out the last vestiges of the original plants around our home. They were installed 11 years ago and the discard pile consisted of 2 white pine trees, 8 mahonia bushes, 12 rug-type juniper bushes and 1 Canadian hemlock tree. They had all mushed together and were no longer attractive.

The basics are these:

Choose and space plants based on what their size will be at maturity, not how big they are now or will grow to be in the next five years. I estimate that most popular landscape plants reach 90 percent of their mature size 5 to 10 years after planting.

When room is especially tight, choose plants that are slow growers or dwarf by nature. This rules out most landscape staples such as common varieties of yew, juniper, arborvitae, spirea and burning bush.

Dwarf or slow-growing varieties of many of these favorites are available. Dwarf lilac, for example, is much better suited to today's landscape than standard types. Some dwarf types have the same richly fragrant blue-purple blossoms clusters found on the huge bushes our great-grandmother grew many years ago.

For evergreen alternatives to common types of yews and junipers, try shrubs like 'Blue Star' juniper, bird's nest spruce, globe spruce and other specialties. 'Blue Star' is a low, compact shrub with steel blue needle color all year, contrasting beautifully with the conventional green growth of other shrubs. It puts on about three inches of outward growth a year. Five of my 'Blue Stars' have been planted four years and are only about 16 inches across.

Bird's nest is one of my all-time favorites because of its shape, slow growth and light-green needle color. It looks like a flattened spruce true and is very dense and symmetrical. Mine are 11 years old and are about 10 inches high and 36 inches across. No pruning has been necessary.

Don't plant slow- and fast-growers near each other. The speedy one will quickly overwhelm the slowpoke. Instead, group shrubs with similar growth patterns together.

Match the plant's need for light with what you have to offer. The quality of light makes a big difference to the plant's long-term health. Example: A dogwood planted in full sun will not do well even if all other conditions are ideal. Dogwood, redbud, serviceberry and a few other spring-blooming trees are called understory trees because they thrive in the filtered light provided by the canopy of tall trees, like oaks, maples, ash and similar hardwoods.

The distinctive shapes of these shrubs have been erased because they've grown together. They should have been spaced further apart.

September's coming – and a great time to repair or start a lawn

The healing time is almost here – four weeks of ideal weather and soil conditions for renovating an existing lawn or starting a new one.

Grass flourishes in the autumn because the weather is even-tempered with ample rain, sunny skies and mild temperatures. The soil is warm and moist and seeds sprout quickly and roots grow vigorously.

At no other time of the year are conditions so perfect. Certainly not in spring when the weather is unpredictable and the soil is chilly and often soggy. Nor in the summer when the midday sun can bake the life out of young, unprotected grass plants.

Here are some suggestions to help you decide what action is needed to take advantage of the prime conditions that September brings most years.

Choosing grass seed – Buy a mixture of types (rye, bluegrass, fescue) that have been blended to match the sunlight and activity conditions that prevail at your home. Mixes are available that run the gamut from sunny to shady and from play to show-piece. Expect to pay about $3 to $5 a pound. Some nurseries offer custom blends formulated for conditions in the particular area.

Preparing the soil – Loosen the top four inches and rake out the top so there are plenty of granules the size of a small marble. The surface should not be glass smooth. Seeds need the protection offered by coarse soil particles. Turning the soil over isn't a good idea because it brings weed seeds to the surface where they will sprout and compete aggressively with your new grass.

A small tiller is useful for loosening the top few inches of soil. Grass seed will sprout better if the soil is loosened and the surface left coarse to provide crevices for seeds to lodge. Shown is the author's brother, Mike Hutchison.

For small areas, several passes with a stiff garden rake loosens the soil sufficiently. Raking works well for large areas, but it is a lot of work. An easier approach is to run a small tiller over the area several times, never pausing long enough for the tines to dig deeper than a few inches into the soil.

Keeping the soil moist – Protect your investment in seed and effort by taking measures to keep the soil moist at all times, especially as the seed is sprouting. Twice-daily mistings may be necessary. A very thin layer of straw spread over the surface helps because it holds it moisture. However, it often contains grain seeds that are a nuisance when they sprout.

Two relatively new products eliminate the need for straw. One is a thin, milky white fabric that, when spread over the seeded area, lets in light, moisture and air. It holds the seed in place and keeps the ground moist. It is similar to landscape fabric used to keep down weeds in the garden and around bushes. Most nurseries carry this product.

The other is a bagged and dry version of the wet hydroseed used by professionals. One popular brand is "Lawn Patch" and it contains seed, fertilizer, mulch and a glue, of sorts, to hold the mix to the ground. It's fluffy out of the bag but when put down and watered in, sticks very well to the ground. It's a good product and comes in blends for sunny or shady areas. This product is widely available at nurseries and home centers.

Feeding the lawn – If you haven't applied fertilizer in the last month or so, do so now and again in late October. The last feeding should be with a blend formulated for fall feeding. The current feeding can be with whatever was used in the spring, providing it contains a blend of nitrogen, phosphorous and potassium.

What's rewarding about fall feeding is that it restores rich, green color to the top and encourages root growth. Roots continue to develop until December, long after top growth has stopped. Turf experts consider fall feeding the most important feeding of the year.

Weeding – Forget crabgrass. It's gone (or is going) to seed now and nothing practical can be done to stop it. Wait until next spring and put down a pre-emergent herbicide that keeps the seeds from sprouting. Other weeds – dandelion, chickweed, plantain and lots of others – can be eradicated with a broadleaf herbicide. Pay attention to the weather since most formulations need 48 rain-free hours to do their job. If you've reseeded, check the label carefully for any cautions about using the product with new grass. It's a good idea to always read and heed label instructions on lawn and garden chemicals.

Starting over – It's a big step but one that should be considered if more than half the lawn is covered with weeds or has only sparse stands of grass. Before plunging in, consult with a local lawn care professional. Techniques such as hydroseeding and slit seeding can restore vigor to an old, tired lawn. For lawns judged beyond repair, the professional with chemicals and machines can usually do a much better job than the homeowner in getting rid of the old lawn and preparing for the new one.

Spring-flowering bulbs earn an E for Easy

If plants were graded like homework, spring-flowering bulbs would earn an E. That's an E for easy, every time.

Tulips, daffodils, hyacinths, crocus and other spring bloomers are among the easiest of plants to grow. Since autumn is the only time to plant them, here is a review of the basics that lead to success:

For the best visual punch, plant bulbs in clusters, rather than a single row. A narrow row strings out the eye while a cluster grabs its attention.

Sally Ferguson, a spokesman for the Dutch bulb industry, takes the cluster approach one step further. She recommends bulbs be planted in a triangular pattern with the long leg of the triangle to the back of the bed. This approach, she said, creates an illusion that more bulbs are planted than actually are.

Group bulbs by the same color, rather than mixing colors in the cluster; again a greater visual impact is gained.

Plant closely. Ferguson recommends spacing tulips, hyacinths and daffodils three to six inches apart. Space smaller bulbs such as crocus, snowdrops, grape hyacinths, one to two inches apart.

Bulbs are at the greatest risk of being dug up by squirrels immediately after they are planted, presumably because the soil is still soft and easily dug by squirrels.

If squirrels are a potential threat in your yard, Ferguson recommends covering the bulbs with a wire mesh like chicken wire before the bulbs are covered back up with soil. The mesh should be large enough to accommodate bulbs' sprouts but not so big that squirrels can easily reach them.

Squirrels tend to favor tulips and crocus over other bulbs; possibly because they taste better. They avoid daffodils, apparently because they taste bad. I don't know if anyone has asked a squirrel which tastes better, much less received an answer, but their preference for tulips and abhorrence for daffodils is fairly well known among bulb growers.

It is easier and quicker to plant a quantity of bulbs if you excavate the entire bulb area rather than dig individual holes. You can space bulbs more uniformly when the whole area is open and this leads to a better-looking bed.

Bulbs should be watered immediately after they are planted. Doing so triggers root growth.

In areas of the country where the first snow can fall as early as Halloween, bulbs are best planted between Sept. 15 and Oct. 15. This period gives the bulb plenty of time to root in before the soil cools, then freezes. Planting in November is better than not planting at all. It is near impossible to store bulbs over the winter, unplanted, and have any luck in planting them next spring.

Spring-flowering bulbs provide the greatest visual punch when planted in clusters of 50 or more bulbs. This beautiful bed of tulips and grape hyacinths was photographed in early May in the Netherlands.

Ferns fade in fall; color, shape and texture on hold

Autumn is a sad time for gardeners who use ferns to bring color, shape and texture to shady areas of the landscape.

The first killing frost usually knocks down the fronds of many ferns that are hardy in the Midwest. Until late next spring when new fiddleheads push through the soil, their presence is sorely missed.

That's how I feel when the ferns disappear for the season from a woody area that separates our yard from the neighbor's. Growing naturally, they provide privacy for both families and do so with charm, thanks to their medium-green, serrated fronds that reach three feet tall.

The ferns in my woodland are of the species Dryopteris. They grow wild in shady areas throughout the Midwest. Some members of the species are evergreen; mine are deciduous and thus at the mercy of autumn frost.

Ferns are not widely planted in home landscapes. That's a shame because they are easy, colorful, multiple readily and bring form and texture that is not found in other plants. They can be used under trees, interspersed in the perennial or annual garden, planted as a ground cover or used as an attractive buffer between a landscaped and woodsy area.

Most share a common need for soil that is on the acidic side, moist and humusy. They do best in deep shade although if the ground is kept moist, some sun is okay. A three-inch blanket of mulch maintained amid a planting will hold in moisture, cool the soil and over time, make the soil more woodland-like.

If the idea of adding ferns to your landscape is appealing, here are some candidates to consider. Each is hardy in the Midwest:

Adiantum – The maidenhair fern. Its foliage is airy, delicate and fan-like. Its 12-inch height makes it excellent for borders; good companion border plants include creeping phlox and lily of the valley.

Athyrium – An exceptionally easy fern and notable for its light green fronds that, despite their height, look graceful and quite at home in shady areas.

Dryopteris – The classic fern because of the serrated edges of its fronds and clump-like habit. Very easy to grow.

Osmunda – Known as the cinnamon fern for the cinnamon color of the fiddleheads. The color changes to dark green as the fronds mature to a height of three feet. As ferns go, this is a relatively slow grower.

Polystichum – Most are evergreen and tend to have long, narrow fronds which form a circular pattern from a central point. These would do really well in low areas of the landscape that are damp and shady, providing the soil is rich and humusy.

It's hard to precisely describe the color, shape and texture of the many worthwhile ferns that can be grown here. For pictures and more information, consult gardening books that focus on shade gardening, ground covers or a book specifically on ferns.

Many local and some mail-order nurseries offer nursery-grown plants, and autumn is a fine time to set out ferns that are growing in pots. Dividing and moving established ferns is a task best left for spring.

Digging from the wild, as was the practice some time ago, is not a good idea because the survival rate is not high and in my opinion, is not environmentally responsible.

Ferns make an excellent visual break between a flower garden and wooded area. Shown is the author's father-in-law, Bill Buchanan, of Jacksonville, Il.

Divide narcissi for years of bountiful blooms

Good things can last a very long time in the garden and fortunately, the narcissi family of spring-flowering bulbs is among those good things.

Daffodils belong to the narcissi group of spring bulbs.

I asked bulb expert Frans M. Roozen how to make narcissi bloom dependably each spring. Roozen lives and works in the bulb growing regions of the Netherlands and is one of the industry's key spokesmen when it comes to technical questions about bulbs.

Here is what he recommends:

Full sun for the eight weeks between the time blooms appear and the time foliage withers is the most important factor in keeping bulbs blooming year after year, he said. During this time the foliage should not be cut, tied, braided or otherwise disturbed.

He cautions against the practice of planting narcissi bulbs in the lawn. While the flowers are lovely as they unfold in the barely-green lawn, the problem begins as grass grows and shades the maturing bulb foliage. He said a better practice that has a similar natural look is to plant narcissi in island beds within the lawn. These can be mowed around, leaving the bulb foliage undisturbed and in full view of the sun.

In beds, you can plant perennials as a way of hiding maturing narcissi foliage. As the perennials emerge, the narcissi foliage will be nearing the end of its eight-week maturation period.

Feeding is another important step. Roozen recommends using a slow-release fertilizer in the fall and in the spring after flowering, feeding with a fertilizer formulated with quick-release nitrogen. Another aid: Mix straw with well-rotted manure and spread it over the bed each fall.

Choosing the right variety is also important. Hundreds of varieties are available and some naturalize better than others, he said. Check the label or catalog for terms like "naturalizing" or "perennializing." This means that particular variety has the genetic potential to multiply readily.

Success at naturalizing does have a pleasant penalty. The penalty is that eventually the bulbs need to be unearthed, baby bulbs separated from the original bulbs and everything replanted.

My experience with narcissi has been that bulbs can go five years before dividing is needed. But this depends so much on how well the bulbs are doing and, especially, how close together they were planted initially that it is hard to be precise. Roozen said that other bulbs that naturalize well (scilla siberica, grape hyacinths, blue bells, snowdrops and eranthis) can be handled the same way.

Whenever the time comes, this is how Roozen said to go about easing the growing pains:

In the spring, note which clumps are overgrown and their location in the yard. Leave them alone for now.

The bulbs will go dormant soon after the foliage has naturally withered; in the Midwest this is usually around mid-June.

When the bulbs are dormant, lift them carefully from the earth and gently separate the new bulbs from the original bulb. They can be replanted immediately or held until autumn in a dry and cool spot. If you choose to replant right away, mix granular slow release fertilizer in with the backfill.

When narcissi bulbs are dormant, lift from the soil and divide. While this task is better done in summer, you can still do so now.

Propagating roses, amaryllis care and more

Another summer has demonstrated that experience is a wonderful teacher when it comes to having a nice yard and garden. Here's a sampling of questions I've been asked recently, and what I hope are useful answers:

Q: My roses are healthy and four years old, but they have not bloomed for two years. Is there anything I can do to make them bloom?

A: Too little sun or too much fertilizer are usually to blame for an otherwise healthy rose bush not blooming. Roses do best in full sun; be wary of shade cast by nearby trees especially as summer progresses and the sun's position shifts. Limit feeding to once monthly. Another culprit: Root stock that has grown from underneath the bud union is often flower-less and for this and other reasons, should be pruned away.

Q: A sprout has appeared on a cut rose I received in an arrangement. I understand if I use a root stimulant and put the stem in the ground and cover it with a quart jar that I can get the start of a rose bush. Does this work?

A: The technique will work; it's the one my grandfather used to add bushes to his collection. The only difference is he took cuttings from garden varieties of roses rather than florist varieties, which are better suited to greenhouse growing.

If you try this technique, do so in early summer with a five-inch cutting taken from the tip of a vigorously growing stem. The glass jar acts as a greenhouse while the stem is rooting. Take care to vent the jar on hot, sunny days. One caution: I believe this practice is illegal on patented rose varieties, unless you have a license to propagate them.

Q: Only one of three roses I planted is growing. Two look brown and dead to me. Could I revive them somehow?

A: If stems are green and supple, the bushes may still be alive and the best tonic is to treat them gently during this period. While they are ailing they won't need any fertilizer and water should be provided to ensure the soil is evenly moist. If the bushes don't leaf out next spring, I'd consider them dead. Roses are best planted in the Midwest in spring or summer.

Q: The amaryllis I received for Christmas last year bloomed beautifully. How can I take care of it so it will bloom again this Christmas?

A: Amaryllis need a few months rest, beginning when the sheath-like leaves wither. While leaves are green, keep the plant watered, fed monthly and situated in a sunny spot. It's okay to set the plant outdoors over summer, providing it is not in direct sun all day.

Leaves usually wither in late summer. When they do, put the bulb (still in the pot is okay) in a cool spot and don't water it. Let it be for six to eight weeks. Growth will begin again when you put it in a sunny spot and water. Water sparingly, keeping the soil barely moist, until leaves are eight inches tall, and then water normally, so the soil is moist.

Q: Should I have my lawn aerated this fall?

A: Aerating a lawn every four years or so is a good practice because it opens up the top few inches of soil, letting air, water and fertilizer reach the grass roots more freely. The machine used for this digs tiny plugs of soil from the top two inches of soil and deposits these plugs on the surface. The plugs can be left in place where they will eventually break apart or they can be raked out.

The durability of amaryllis can be seen by this bulb's vigorous growth in its shipping bag, without soil. Far better for the amaryllis' longevity to pot the bulb, enjoy its bloom and then let it recycle for another round of blossoms.

Chilly? So what. Keep on gardening

Ignore the chill in the air. Sure, winter's coming and there are things to do because of it, but it's too early to abandon the garden for the easy chair.

Here are some ideas to help stretch the season:

Unlike most summer flowers that die at first frost, geraniums will keep blooming providing they are kept healthy. This means feeding every other week, watering regularly and keeping spent flowers picked. Give them as much full sun as possible. One of the resort hotels on Mackinaw Island in Northern Michigan routinely has geraniums in bloom well into November. While weather conditions are ideal there because of the moderating effects of Lakes Michigan and Huron, the groundkeeper's success demonstrates that geraniums are a dependable long-season plant.

Snapdragons, pansies and calendula that have stood still over summer are revived by mellow autumn weather. Feed these, too, to keep blossoms coming. Pansies will withstand light frost. Some garden centers have fresh crops of pansies available now. Plant them now to enjoy their autumn flowers, then cover with leaves over winter. Chances are, they'll survive winter and bloom gloriously from May to June next spring.

Pansies are a wonderful companion plant with spring bulbs, especially daffodils, because their flower shape, size and coloration contrast beautifully. Pansy foliage also is handy for hiding bulb foliage as it matures into early summer.

Look to garden asters and mums for autumn color. Both are available as potted plants at many garden centers. Asters are becoming increasingly popular because of their vivid yet soft blossom color and shape. Like mums, they can be wintered over to enjoy next year. A mulch of leaves heaped around the withered foliage and stems helps pull them through cold and snowy winters.

Flowering kale and cabbage provide excellent autumn color. Flowering is a misnomer as both are grown for their large, colorful and fancy-edged foliage. Some have an upright shape while other types are flatter, like a conventional garden cabbage. Plant these in the ground or put some in a decorative pot on the front step or patio. They'll look good even when covered with snow, so resilient is the foliage and its coloration. Look for both as potted plants in garden centers.

While you are busy enjoying your autumn garden, do take some time to ready it for winter. Among the tasks are these:

- Remove suckers from the base of crabapple trees, rose bushes and other shrubs. Ideally these are removed when first seen but getting them out now will help the plant direct its spring vigor usefully.

- Divide perennials now. Most are easily divided by lifting the root ball from the soil and splitting the mass in two or more pieces with a sharp spade. Remove any unhealthy or damaged parts. Before replanting the pieces, work some compost or sphagnum peat moss into the soil to create a friendly root zone. Water the divisions right after planting and again every week till the ground freezes. At this point, it helps to mulch the roots with leaves or compost to help prevent the roots from being tossed from the soil during freeze-thaw cycles.

An exception: Leave healthy peonies alone. If conditions are right, they will thrive 20 or more years without dividing. If they are not blooming, it probably means they are not getting the full sun they need or the roots are set at an incorrect depth. If either condition applies to your peonies, then lift them now and replant in a rich, loamy soil. Eyes on the root should be set about two inches below the surface.

Healthy geraniums planted in containers or the garden can provide glorious color until late in the fall.

No lilies in the garden? You're missing a lot of color!

Gardeners get passionate about a lot of things they grow, but lilies seldom make the list. For many, this romance begins and ends with a potted Easter lily.

I'm as guilty as anyone, having waited 35 years to plant my first lily bulb. That was several years ago and I now have an inkling of what I missed all those years.

I missed a plant with blossoms that almost make a round trip around the color wheel – pure white, creams, yellows, oranges, golds, pinks and reds. Some are clear colors while others are spotted or textured. Some are richly fragrant, filling a garden or room with perfume. Others have little fragrance.

I missed a plant that mixes superbly with annuals, perennials, evergreens and leafy shrubs, a plant with varieties that bloom June to October in most parts of the country. In other words, I missed a lot of flower power over the years.

The good news is that autumn is an excellent time to make up for this omission. The lily is one of the few if not the only bulbs that can be planted in either autumn or spring. Autumn is preferred and when planted now, some will send up a few leaf sprouts as their roots settle in.

Here's a look at the five major types:

Oriental lilies – Big flowers on 36-inch stems, strong colors and rich fragrance are characteristic of this group, which blooms from mid-June through late September. The pure white, textured flower of L. 'Casa Blanca' is sweetly and deeply fragrant; I can detect its fragrance from 30 feet. Other gems: L. speciosum 'Rubrum' and L. 'Stargazer.'

Trumpet lilies – The Easter lily is a trumpet type. In the garden, blossoms first appear in early July and continue through mid-August. Colors run from pure white, to creams to pinks and yellow and are borne on 60- to 72-inch stems, making this an ideal back row plant. Once established, most varieties produce 18-30 buds on a stem with several open at any one time.

Tiger lilies – A tough, vigorous plant remembered for its abundance of vivid orange blossoms in mid-summer. Breeders have ventured in and given this tiger new stripes and manners. Look for hybrids in shades of peach-pink, soft pink, apple blossom pink and similar pastels, many spotted with black or dark brown specks. Blossoms July-August and grows three to five feet tall.

Asiatic lilies – Blooming during July and August, this is the free-spirited lily group with blossoms varying in shape from plain, open bowls to those with delicate petals arranged in a formal star pattern. Colors range from soft pastels to intense reds and oranges. Shorter than most at 24-36 inches.

Lilies are one of the stars of the summer garden and the magnificent Asiatic hybrids are among the most popular among American gardeners because of their excellent color, foliage and vigor. (Photo courtesy Netherlands Flower Bulb Information Center)

Species lilies – In a sense, these are the original lilies. It is with these that breeders begin their work. This group is more varied (two to six feet) in height and bloom time (late May to September) than hybrids. Since they are "closer to nature" than the hybrids, they tend to be hardier and more pest resistance. Some of the most useful in this group include the white Madonna lily (L. candidum) and the pink Turk's cap lily (L. martagon).

Lilies like soil and weather conditions that come natural in many parts of the country or are easy to provide. They do best in well-drained, loamy soil with full morning sun and protection from mid-day sun. Soil that is light or heavy can be improved by working one part compost or sphagnum peat moss to three parts native soil into the hole at planting time.

Generally, lilies are pest-free. Aphids and other insects are easily eradicated with insecticides, and leafspot disease, prevalent on some varieties, can be kept in check with fungicide.

Rabbits and rodents are more of a problem than insects and disease. Moles, mice and similar critters that feed on the bulb can be discouraged by treating the bulbs with a dusting powder before planting, and rabbits, by treating emerging shoots with a spray-on repellent. As with any garden chemical, please read and follow label instructions.

Tackle the little chores while weather's still good

Procrastinators, October is your opportunity to do stuff in the yard that you've been putting off since Labor Day.

But autumn's golden growing moments are fleeting, so act fast. Based on questions I'm asked most autumns, here's a cornucopia of autumn things to act on – now!

- Repair dead or weak patches in the lawn by sowing grass seed after you've worked the soil surface to a coarse texture. How much sprouts and how big it gets depends a lot on the weather, but at least it will have a start on next spring.

- Cut back or restrain long canes of climbing roses that would otherwise by whipped by winter wind. Take as little cane length as necessary as climbing roses set flower on mature wood, as well as new growth. If you choose the restrain route, use something that will not cut into the canes.

- Provide water to rhododendron, holly and other broadleaf evergreen bushes weekly until the ground freezes, unless there's plenty of rain. These shrubs need an ample supply of water to withstand the drying effects of winter wind and sun.

- Prevent squirrels from digging up newly planted bulbs by covering them top and sides with a piece of hardware cloth (chicken wire) before backfilling the hole. Don't leave bulb skins — called tunics — on top of the soil after planting as this debris attracts squirrels and seems to make them pursue the bulbs you've just planted.

- Determine what's needed to winterize fish and plants in ponds. In freezing climates, fish will do fine over winter if the pond is kept at least partially open. If it freezes over, there is little or no exchange of gasses, a situation that harms fish and plants. Small and efficient electric heaters will keep ponds open sufficiently to keep fish alive. Or, fish can be kept in an aquarium indoors properly sized and equipped.

Perennial water lilies can be overwintered indoors in a bucket of water. For these, allow the foliage to die back and the plant to go dormant before bringing it indoors to store in a cool, dark spot. Water lilies in ponds deeper than three feet can be left in the bottom of the pond over winter. Many other plants grown in ponds located in areas of the country that experience prolonged freezing temperatures are best treated as annuals, in my opinion. Water gardening has grown to become a popular and exacting hobby. For detailed information, please consult a reference book dedicated to that subject.

Before winter sets in, determine what water garden plants should be brought in for the winter. Some are best treated as annuals in cold climates.

- If moles have been a problem, repair the damage to your yard, but don't worry about the moles for now as they are difficult to locate now because of the changes in their feeding habits. Next spring, you can take steps to make your yard an undesirable feeding ground.

  There are lots of remedies and the best I've found are products based on castor oil. These liquid concentrates are sprayed on the yard and moles find the taste on their fur and insects they eat unpalatable. It doesn't harm the moles, but it does send them elsewhere for an untainted food source. Look for it at nurseries and the garden department of home centers.

- Enjoy garden color for several more weeks by planting sedum, flowering kale and cabbage, garden mums and pansies. Each can withstand frost. Sedum is a perennial especially prized for its autumn color. Pansies, too, will overwinter, especially if covered late in the autumn with a blanket of leaves. They'll bloom next spring.

- Garden mums are best protected over winter by mounding leaves on the plant after the weather has turned cold for good, which usually occurs in the Midwest around Thanksgiving. Don't cut back the plant's stems as they will hold the leaf mulch in place.

Save time and sweat: Mow, don't rake, leaves

No, you don't have to rake your leaves.

Mulch 'em up with your lawnmower instead.

Research at Michigan State University (MSU), East Lansing, continues to demonstrate that the lawnmower and not the rake is the tool of choice for homeowners anxious to make quick work of leaf disposal. Any mower will work; it is not necessary to have a mulching model.

MSU turfgrass expert Dr. Paul Rieke offers four easy tips for the homeowner interested in this labor-saving technique: Sharpen the mower's blade. Mow when leaves are dry. Make several passes with the mower, rather than one. And make sure grass tips are not covered by mulched leaves so photosynthesis can continue.

"We've successfully mulched a layer of leaves 16 inches deep and the only detrimental effect was a slight thinning of the turf. Mowing a layer six to eight inches deep would be no problem for the lawn," he said.

Researchers at MSU's Turfgrass Center began their investigation in the mid-1990s and data continues to support early findings that mowing is an efficient way to dispose of leaves. The mulched leaves appear to have no effect on soil fertility or structure.

Recent work suggests this technique works best on lawns in sunny areas and that much of the mulched layer decomposes before the lawn greens up in the spring, Rieke said.

That mulched leaves decompose at a time of the year when compost piles stand still can be explained.

"The soil remains warm and moist even though the air temperature has cooled considerably. Warm, moist soil favors the work of microbes, which are responsible for breaking down the leaves," Rieke noted.

Why don't leaves add to the fertility and structure of the soil? Rieke said researchers now believe that the benign effect of mulched leaves can be attributed to the relatively low volume of material that is added to the soil. In other words, there's not enough leaf material introduced to the soil to make any notable difference, especially over a period of several years.

"What will be interesting will be at what point mulched leaves have an impact on the soil," he said. "It could be many years before this effect is seen."

One pass with the lawn mower reduced this handful of leaves to half their original size. Another pass will reduce size further and speed decomposition.

Plant trees now for a jump start next spring

It's true that autumn is a great time to plant most trees, shrubs and perennials.

But what about when autumn begins to feel like winter? Should the gardener trade shovel for shawl and begin hibernating? Maybe, especially when Halloween rolls around.

Evergreen trees (spruce, pine and the like) should be planted by the first of November. This is so roots will have enough time to acclimate to their new surroundings before soil cools. A modestly established root system will be better able to draw water from the soil and replenish moisture lost through the needles.

On the other hand, most deciduous trees can be planted until the time the ground freezes. The difference in timing is that a leafless tree does not lose moisture like an evergreen.

Some nurseries offer autumn tag and plant programs. These programs let the gardener choose a tree during fall color. The tree is left in the field until it goes dormant weeks later and is then harvested by the nursery and planted by the consumer. This lets the gardener get a jump on next year's growing season. Survival rate is excellent providing the tree is planted properly and watered.

Proper planting means preparing a proper hole and the current recommendation is that the hole be only as deep as the root ball but twice as wide. Wide, not deep, gives the trees' roots an opportunity to stretch out and get established before sinking tap-like roots.

Depending on the species chosen and the nursery's experience, other practices help ensure winter survival and robust spring green-up. Check with your nurseryman to see if these guidelines apply:

Water deeply, weekly, until the ground freezes.

Do not over-enrich the backfill. If the native soil has a lot of sand or clay, add no more than 25 percent compost, sphagnum peat moss or a similar amendment. A too-rich root zone soil blend encourages lazy roots that ultimately strangle themselves.

Stake the tree, especially if it is planted in an exposed or windy location. Three stakes and anchoring wire are usually sufficient. Do not have the wire exposed to the trunk, otherwise it will cut into it and severe damage to the tree can result. Thread wire through short sections of old garden hose, plastic tubing or a similar material to protect the trunk from the wire.

Mulch the root zone with compost, fallen leaves or shredded bark, but wait to do so until the ground has frozen hard. Do not place the mulch directly against the trunk. Spread out in the root area, the mulch will provide a more mellow soil environment for the roots as they establish themselves.

Better wider than deeper for the planting hole, as the author demonstrates with a weeping cherry. Current nursery industry thinking is the hole should be only as deep as the root ball but twice again as wide.

Container plantings need extra care over winter

Overwintering pot-bound small shrubs and trees is a challenge but can be accomplished with a bit of effort and luck.

Now's the time to put forth the effort – and hope for the luck.

The challenge lies in protecting the root ball from severe cold. In the ground, there's protection and moisture from the soil mass. However, the container is isolated from the protective mass of the ground soil. Since it's exposed to wind and cold on all sides and top, it quickly freezes and stays that way.

I've been successful in keeping potted specimen plants alive over winter by sheltering the planters in the garage where there's protection from sun and wind and where the air temperature is a bit warmer. While the soil still freezes in January and February, it is possible to add water to the soil to replace what has been loss through normal transpiration.

I'm not certain if daylight has contributed to my overwintering success, but I do put the planters close to the north-facing windows where they get light, weak though it is. To date, I've pulled potted miniature tree roses, dwarf evergreens and a holly bush through the winter using this technique. But these were the lucky ones; other winters I've lost similar plants using the same technique.

If your potted tree or shrub is too big or heavy to bring into the garage, there are a few things that can be done to protect it.

The first is to surround the root ball with an insulating material. Bales of straw work well but look tacky. A slightly more pleasant sight is straw or leaves packed tight in clear plastic bags, snuggled against the root area of the container. If possible, move the pot out of the open and up against the house, garage or even a fence. Anything to block wind and sun will help.

If the plant is an evergreen, spray it with an anti-dessicant in November and again on a warm day in January or February. These materials protect plants by coating the stems, leaves and branches with a wax-like layer that lets the plant breathe but stops excess loss of moisture. This won't do much good for a deciduous shrub since without leaves, there is little chance of moisture loss.

A screen of burlap around the pot will also reduce damage from sun and wind. Secure the burlap with stakes installed in the container, before the soil freezes. Space the burlap so it doesn't rub against the plant.

About the only other thing you can do is to periodically water the plant, especially if it's an evergreen. Chances are there will be warm spells every several weeks at which point a few quarts of lukewarm water will be nicely absorbed by the crusty container soil and most welcomed by the plant.

Most container materials – plastic and wood – are not harmed by winter sun and general weathering. They'll deteriorate a bit but not destructively so. The exception is terra cotta. It is highly prone to cracking over winter so it is best brought into the garage or a similar protected location.

Dwarf evergreens and other specimen plants are great in containers but require special protection over winter.

Tulips and hyacinths abound in this outdoor lasagna

Feeling adventuresome and willing to push your green thumb a bit? Want to aim for something beautiful, knowing that success is not entirely within your control?

If so, then try your hand at growing a layered mix of spring-flowering bulbs in containers to enjoy on the patio, front step or most anywhere else. All it takes is a container, soil, bulbs, a little work and some luck that the winter won't be too hard.

Risk aside, it's like making lasagna, but instead of pasta, cheese and meat, different types of bulbs are arranged in layers of soil that fill the container.

To create a splashy show, the container should be at least 12 inches deep, 15 inches across and have drainage holes for excess water to drain away. Old whiskey half-barrels or similar wooden containers work well because they are typically big enough and proportioned nicely. Plastic containers are iffy because they can crack when it's really cold. Containers made from terra cotta should not be used because they are very likely to crack in sub-freezing temperatures.

For soil, blend your own, mixing equal parts garden soil, perlite (or vermiculite), sphagnum peat moss and coarse sand. This creates a fairly light, quick-to-drain mix. Or, you could use a commercial potting soil if you don't want to bother with the homemade. Soil from the garden seldom provides the sharp drainage needed in a container, so it's best to avoid it.

The lasagna approach comes in layering of the bulbs. Plant lots of bulbs close together on each layer for the most dramatic color. Bulbs can touch each other, but should not touch the side of the container.

Tall-growing bulbs such as tulips or daffodils, or both, should be planted eight inches deep and covered with three inches of soil. An intermediate layer of hyacinths can be added now and topped with one inch of soil. For the final layer, use low-growing bulbs such as grape hyacinths or crocus. Cover this top layer with four inches of soil and finally, an inch of mulch. Shredded bark, wood chips or chopped-up leaves work fine as a mulch. Water well.

Almost any bulb will work well. When choosing, consider blooming period, color, height and fragrance and plant what meets your fancy. A tub that includes hyacinths is especially welcome where there is a window nearby that can be opened to enjoy their fragrance.

And now for the tricky part.

Bulbs need at least 15 weeks of cold, but not freezing cold, to root and prepare for blooming. Bulbs in containers are much more susceptible to extreme cold than those in the ground. The soil in the containers provides some insulation, but often it's not enough in normal winters, much less really cold ones.

Adequate protection can be provided by storing the containers in a sheltered area or an unheated garage or shed. Even though temps drop below freezing, the soil in the container should provide enough insulation if the container is protected. The container can be moved to its show place position in early spring, after temperatures have moderated.

Having to move the container to a protected area, then out again, forces some limitation on the size of the container because of its loaded weight. Containers with soil can easily weigh 50 pounds of more and that's a lot of dead weight to be moving about. Containers that are too heavy to be moved can be wrapped in padded burlap or plastic blister wrap, or even surrounded by bales of straw, to keep them from freezing.

What about planting bulbs in window boxes? That's asking for disappointment, in my opinion. Window boxes tend to be narrow and shallow and there's not a lot of soil to begin with, much less extra to provide thermal protection. It might be worth a try, though, if the window box is in a very protected location.

If you want to try any of these lasagna approaches to bulbs in containers, good luck – and here's hoping winter won't be too tough on the bulbs, or us, when you take the plunge.

Bulbs can be layered in large containers to provide a splashy show of color next spring. (illustration courtesy Netherlands Flower Bulb Information Center)

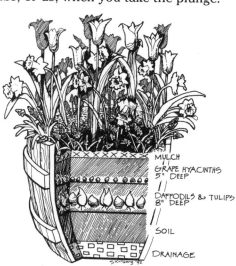

MULCH

GRAPE HYACINTHS
5" DEEP

DAFFODILS & TULIPS
8" DEEP

SOIL

DRAINAGE

Look around – did pests get the best of your garden?

With the growing season essentially over, now is a good time to assess the damage insects, disease, animals and weeds caused your landscape and the plants in it.

Damage from deer and moles and problems with roses, tomatoes and annual flowers seem to be perennial favorites. Here's a look at these, plus another approach that may relieve anxiety if you score your gardening success less than perfect.

Deer continue to cause massive damage to shrubs, trees and garden plants, especially among gardeners living in rural or heavily wooded areas. Other than elimination of the herd in your locale, there is no sure-fire solution I'm aware of. There are repellents that can be sprayed on foliage, high-frequency sound generators, fencing and a host of home-grown remedies aimed at keeping deer away or discouraging them from feeding.

Fencing offers the best hope, but can be impractical or unsightly, not to mention expensive and easy to penetrate if a gate is left open. One point of relief may be a plastic grid fence marketed by Benner's Gardens, Inc., of New Hope, Penn. It is extremely strong and once installed, essentially invisible given its dark green color. If I had a garden or wooded area I was willing to enclose, it would be with this material. Cost ranges from $.60 to $1 a linear foot.

Moles are a significant problem for many gardeners, especially those living near wooded areas where humusy soil is rich with insects and easy for burrowing. Cats do a good job eradicating a mole once it surfaces. For cat-less gardeners, two products offer hope. One is a soil insecticide tradenamed Merit. It gets rid of grubs that moles feed on.

The other is a spray-on product called Mole-Med. It leaves a castor oil residue on soil insects and the mole, neither of which the mole apparently likes, and it leaves the area because of it. University research shows Mole-Med and a similar product called Scoot-Mole keeps moles away for up to 10 weeks.

Blackspot and mildew continue to be a problem among the 30 rose bushes in my garden. Damp weather, poor air circulation among bushes and too little sun favor these diseases. My problems can be traced to two mistakes: Not using more than one of the fungicides labeled for this problem and starting treatment too late.

Couple that with a rose bed that's grown shady over the years as nearby trees grew, it's not hard to see why there's a problem. One solution: Move the bushes to where there's more sun and air movement and use different chemistries of fungicides.

Disease on tomatoes bothers lots of gardeners. Two things can help. One is to rotate where in the garden tomatoes are planted and the other is to choose varieties that are resistant to disease. Disease resistance is indicated by abbreviations on the seed packet or plant label. The more sets of abbreviations, the more resistant that variety.

Planting the same thing in the same spot can be a problem for annual flowers, too. Nutrients in the soil can be depleted and soil-borne disease can flourish from same plant-same spot practices. A lot of substitutions are possible to break this cycle. Here are some plant pairs that, among varieties available, offer similar growth habits, flower colors and sun requirement:

Nicotiana for petunias, dahlias for zinnias, salvia for snapdragons, phlox for alyssum, browallia for impatiens and wax begonias and cosmos for geraniums.

Left unchecked, blackspot weakens a rose bush by causing excessive leaf drop.

Tidy up the garden before all becomes mush

Lots of things improve with age but one that doesn't is dead plant foliage. It grows more disgusting every day.

Consider this observation a gentle reminder to clean up your garden before late autumn weather makes doing so unbearable.

A few weeks ago I sized up the hosta plants in my yard and the withering foliage that remained of an otherwise colorful season. The procrastinator in me said, "Wait, the leaves are still making food. It's too early to cut them back." Then, the "seize the moment" muse took control and I cut 'em back, cleanly and crisply, with no mushy green stuff to deal with later.

Now, before the cold and snowy-rain precipitation of late autumn makes it any more messy than it already is, prowl your yard looking for stuff to tidy up. Here's a look at places and things to consider.

Fallen apples are a nuisance because they're slippery to walk over and messy chopped up in a lawn mower. They are an important link in the life cycle of the apple maggot, a nasty bug that leaves the skin pockmarked and the flesh brown-streaked and unappealing.

By the time an infested apple falls – and it usually does so before it's ripe – the damage to that year's crop has been done. Chemical controls next year will help but even a better way is to get rid of the fallen fruit now, before winter sets in. Pick up fruits as they fall since the immature maggot typically crawls out within a week of the fruit falling to the ground. It wastes no time getting to work.

Cool, damp autumn nights take their toll on roses, disfiguring the leaves with a white, powdery mildew or an irregular dark spot called black spot. Leaves infected with either cannot be saved – once the disease is apparent it is too late to do anything about the leaf.

What should be done, though, is to remove any diseased leaves. Often, these leaves will be at the base of the plant where moisture is high and air movement low. It's the base that needs winter protection (not before mid-November) and if the gardener buries diseased leaves while covering the plant, the spores will winter over and can severely damage next spring's foliage.

Perennial foliage should be removed with a sharp knife or pruning shears at ground level. Cut it cleanly; pulling on the mushy stems could damage the roots. Annuals can be yanked out of the soil and are easier to remove before repeated frosts turn the stems mushy. Any seed pods left on annuals, like marigold, salvia, zinnia and others, are not worth saving now because fall rains and high humidity have likely zapped the seeds' vitality.

Some perennial plants should be carefully removed from the garden and stored inside. These include tuberous-rooted begonias, dahlias and caladiums. Frost quickly nips their foliage, but does not harm the root. Gently dig the root and rinse with tap water. Dry it in a cool and airy spot for a few days and then store loosely in a plastic tub filled with perlite, vermiculite or dry peat moss. Keep the tub in a cool (45 to 55 degrees) dry room away from light.

There are a few maintenance chores that should not be done now. Don't prune trees like oak, maple, ash, locust and others that are dropping leaves. They are not yet dormant. Don't do any major pruning of evergreens like yews or junipers. Touch them up if they're blocking a walkway or will be damaged by snow, but don't do much to them now.

Mush comes next: Frost has zapped these impatiens; it's a lot easier and cleaner to remove them quickly than to wait until cold weather turns them to mush.

Bulbs left to plant? Get 'em in the ground now

Here's a gardener's dilemma to ponder: "Do I dare plant spring-flowering bulbs this late in the season?"

The gamble is this: Spring bulbs need six weeks to root before the ground freezes. The ground is warmer than the air, but is there enough time for adequate rooting to occur before the ground freezes shut?

It's an iffy gamble but one worth taking for two reasons, especially with minor bulbs: Minor bulbs are inexpensive and the bright blossom color they bring in late winter combine to make the risk worth taking.

Crocus is the best known and widely grown of these bulbs because it is widely available, inexpensive, colorful (purple, yellow, white and striped) and comes up vigorously year after year. The bulbs multiple each year, making even a modest planting of a few hundred bulbs more beautiful as the years pass. Cold spring weather doesn't hurt the leaves or flowers, no matter their stage of growth.

Most other minor bulbs share the crocus' good points of color, early bloom and hardiness. Among candidates to consider for planting now – late as it is – are these:

Chionodoxa goes by the common name, Glory of the Snow. This native of the mountains of Asia Minor is very hardy and blooms just as crocus are finishing. The flower is star-shaped and resembles a tiny daylily blossom. Several good varieties include 'Luciliae,' (bright blue with white centers); 'Albae,' (white) and 'Rosea' (pink-lilac). The flowers are borne singly on stems about six inches long. 'Gigantea' has flowers on 10-inch stems in purple, pink or white.

Galanthus, or snowdrop, usually blossoms just before crocus. It is an extremely long-lived bulb; plantings can last for decades. 'Nivalis' has bell-shaped flowers on stems 6 to 9 inches long. 'Elwesii' stems are 12 inches. Flowers of both are waxy white and green-tipped inside.

Muscari, or grape hyacinth, has grass-like foliage that can look untidy in the garden. But the sweet fragrance of the flowers more than makes up for that misgiving. Popular varieties include 'Armeniacum,' a bright-blue flower on stems 4 to 8 inches long, and 'Botryoides,' a deep-blue flower on stems 6 to 12 inches long. An unusual variety is 'Monstrosum,' with its fuzzy, marine-blue flower.

Scilla is typically called squill flower. Most varieties bear several bell-shaped flowers an inch or so across on stems under eight inches tall. An outstanding variety is 'Bifolia.' It bears six to eight flowers on eight-inch stems and is available in turquoise, white, violet and pink. 'Siberica' has sky-blue flowers on stems three to six inches long.

Anemone (windflower) blooms in mid- to late-spring and most varieties bear flowers one inch across on stems six to nine inches long. Colors are exceptionally bright and clear and include shades of lavender, blue and pink.

Generally, these bulbs do best when planted in a sunny spot and well-drained soil. Light shade is okay. Because they bloom so early (March-April), withering foliage should not be an obstacle to planting the summer garden.

The key to enjoying the minor bulb is simple: Plant a lot and plant in clusters. Since the flowers are small and are not readily seen from the street, plant the bulbs within eyesight of the kitchen or family room windows where you can see and enjoy them.

Among spring-flowering bulbs, Galanthus is notable for its courage to bloom while there's snow on the ground. Pictured is the variety 'Nivalis.' (Photo courtesy Netherlands Flower Bulb Information Center)

Hurry spring by forcing bulbs to bloom indoors

All eyes will soon turn to the poinsettia as the holiday plant of the moment. And what a moment it is, given the modern poinsettia's ability to look good for two months or longer.

But this is not a story about poinsettias. It's about bulbs and it's meant as a reminder that you can easily grow a crop of spring-flowering bulbs in your home by taking a few steps now. Here's the scoop:

Growing a pot of daffodils is about as easy as opening a can of soup. All it takes is a few bulbs, a shallow pan, a few cup fulls of gravel, a few quarts of water and about six weeks to bring them into flower.

Daffodils blooming before winter snow melts may not suit everyone's taste, yet the technique used to bring them to flower indoors is the same that coaxes tulips, hyacinths, crocus and other bulbs into early, early bloom indoors. The practice is called forcing. The gardener provides the cool temperatures needed to trigger growth. This artificial winter is far shorter than nature's.

Popular forcing bulbs like tulips and hyacinths require a resting period of 10 to 15 weeks during which roots develop. The potted bulbs should be stored where neither mice nor frost can reach them; a temperature range of 38 to 50 degrees is ideal. Good locations include the basement, garage, crawl space, shed or, ideally, a root cellar.

The next step is a one- or two-week stay in a location that gets direct sun or fluorescent light but is cool, 50 to 55 degrees. The last step is to bring the pot to a sunny window or under fluorescent lights where buds will continue to develop and quickly open. Temperatures shouldn't exceed 70 degrees for hyacinths, 65 for daffodils and tulips and 55 for crocus, freesia and tulips of the Kaufmanniana and Gregii types. Warmer temperatures shorten the flower's life.

Daffodils are easiest and quickest. Since they are from the Mediterranean area, they don't require a cooling period. They can be grown in a shallow (two to four inch) deep container filled with pebbles or small stones. To begin, fill the dish half full with pebbles and gently place the bulbs on the surface. Surround the bulbs with enough pebbles to hold them in place and fill the container with water to a level just below the top of the stones.

After planting, set the container in a cool (50 degrees) and dark area. The roots will develop in about three weeks and the container can be moved to a sunny window as sprouts appear. Don't let the temperature exceed 70 degrees and keep the water level just below the bulbs.

Tulips and hyacinths require a longer cooler period and should be potted in a deeper container filled with a loose houseplant mix or a blend of peat moss and either coarse sand or perlite. Water after potting and then keep the soil sparsely moist while rooting proceeds.

Pre-cooled hyacinth bulbs are also available. These root quickly in water and come into blossom a few weeks later. The easiest way to do this is with a specially designed hyacinth glass that holds and supports the bulb just so.

Don't scrimp on either bulb size or rooting time. Whenever possible, buy the largest bulb possible. If the store bin or catalog says "Forcing size," so much the better. Expect to pay $1 for top-sized tulip and daffodils bulbs and $1.50 or more for hyacinths. Don't rush the rooting time. Twelve weeks is a good average and it won't hurt the bulbs to keep them in the rooting cycle a few weeks longer.

Hyacinths root and blossom quickly when "planted" in a hyacinth glass. (Photo courtesy Netherland Flower Bulb Information Center)

Yes, Virginia, the Christmas cactus really is a cactus

Cacti and desert go hand-in-hand, making it hard to visualize a pint-sized Christmas cactus blooming alongside a giant Saguaro in the Sonoran Desert.

Does this suggest the Christmas cactus is something else? Years of bogus botany handed down among generations of houseplant fans?

Rest easy. The Christmas cactus is a true cactus. Ditto for its Thanksgiving and Easter cousins. Botanists classify plants not by the shape or size of the plant but by its flower, and sure enough, the flowers of the Christmas cactus are structurally similar to that of the Saguaro and other desert-dwellers.

Brazilian rain forests are the native habitat of Christmas cacti where they thrive up in the trees, rather than on the ground.

That's one tidbit for you. Here's another, and it's sure to dazzle your friends: What is the difference among Thanksgiving, Christmas and Easter-blooming cacti? The answer:

- Thanksgiving cacti have several sharp edges on the margins of stem segments and blooms are almost always at the end of the stem.

- Christmas cacti have scalloped edges, and blooms, too, are mostly at the end of each stem.

- Easter cacti have flowers between the stem segments and the ends.

Now you know!

You probably already know how easy these plants are to care for and if you've been in a store lately, how plentiful they are now. Here's a refresher on shopping and care:

- Choose a plant with plump, ready-to-open buds. Tiny buds may fall off because of the sudden change in environment from the greenhouse to your home.

- Avoid plants with puckered or off-colored stems. These are signs the plant has received too much or too little water.

- Normal home temperatures are just fine.

- Put it by a window bright enough to read the newspaper by. Or, if you want it to brighten a dark corner, that's fine. It should have enough bud-power to bloom three weeks, even if the light isn't to its liking.

- For watering purposes, pretend it is not a cactus. Water it when the top inch of potting soil is dry. It will take less water than green foliage plants, poinsettias or African violets. Better to water less than more.

- After blooms are gone, pinch back a stem segment or two. This will force out new growth and that means more flowers.

- How much light a Christmas cactus should get during its non-blooming time is a subject of debate. I've had good luck by putting the plant in a sunny window, pulling it back slightly during the height of the summer when the sun is especially intense.

As to feeding, I use houseplant fertilizer from spring to late summer, when the plant is putting out most of its new growth. As with any garden chemical, please read and heed the instructions on the fertilizer label.

Sharp edges on the stems and blooms at the end of the stem mean this plant is a Thanksgiving cactus.

Put genetics and microclimates to your advantage

Some of the gardening chores that typically occur during the nasty weather of late autumn may not be necessary – things like screening rhododendrons, protecting roses and the like.

The winter hardiness of a given plant and its overall performance depends a lot on its genes and the climate immediately surrounding the plant. You can make these work for you, but it takes advance planning. Here are some things to consider as you plan and plant:

Plant expedition and breeding programs are underway to either find or develop plants that do not require protection yet look great in the landscape. The University of Minnesota, for example, is making excellent progress in developing strains of cold-hardy plants.

Roses are a good example. Virtually all modern hybrid roses require some form of winter protection. Many of the old-fashioned varieties do not require protection, nor do the new landscape or shrub types. If you like roses but don't want the mess and work involved in protecting them over winter, these types are for you. As an added bonus, blossoms of many of the old varieties are wonderfully fragrant and gracefully shaped. The bushes tend to have the same insect and disease problems of modern varieties, however.

Other types of super-hardy woody shrubs and trees are on the market now, and from what I read, many more are under development. Local nurseries and mail-order specialists are the best place to find plants of this nature. This is different than choosing a plant that matches the local hardiness zone, as mapped by the United States Department of Agriculture. What we're talking about here is choosing a plant that has been developed, or found and brought to market, because of its super winter hardiness.

You can also avoid the hassle of providing winter protection by using natural or humanmade microclimates. This is a place in your yard that is warmer and less windy than other places. A few extra degrees and less wind can make a big difference to the plant's overall vigor.

A Japanese maple is growing very well in my yard, in part because it is protected from winter wind. It was planted in 1990 in a protected "L" created by the garage and back of the house. Had the tree been planted six feet away, it would have been in the wind's way and screening would have been needed to protect it. I didn't want to look at a burlap screen all winter, or have the hassle of putting it up and taking it down.

Late autumn is a good time to look for these areas in your yard. Then, come spring, you can add plants that take advantage of the more gentle nature of the area. Here are some things to watch for:

- What areas are already protected from the prevailing winds, especially winter wind? Such areas are usually warmer in the winter; do you recall them as hot and dry in the summer? If so, that could require more water or mulching to compensate.

- What areas can be made more gentle by erecting a fence to serve as a landscape accent and windbreak? Are there unplanted areas, such as around the "L" of your home, that would look nicer with trees and shrubs?

- What areas offer a canopy of protection from the summer sun and wind? This could be as simple as a grouping of pine trees that provide ideal climatic and other conditions for rhododendrons, azaleas, pieris, mahonia and other broadleaf evergreens.

This Japanese maple does very well, in part, because it's protected from prevailing winter wind. Conditions just a few feet away are far more harsh.

Harvest fresh holiday decorating materials from your yard

Decorating the house for Christmas a few hundred years ago meant using natural materials that could easily spoil in just a few days.

Colonial decorating is still practiced at Colonial Williamsburg (CW) in Williamsburg, Va., and the staff there continues to be challenged by the need to keep things looking nice throughout the holiday weeks. When weather turns warm, apples, oranges and other fruits used indoors begin to drip and spoil.

"Watch and replace" seems to be CW's unspoken motto in this regard and it's equally apt for decorators elsewhere. Here are some tips to help you select and enjoy the beauty that comes from natural materials:

- Apples, oranges and other fresh fruits begin to spoil when the flesh is pierced in preparation for attaching it to a wreath or other frame. If there's some other way to attach it, choose that method. This is less a problem outside where cooler temperatures slow down deterioration. Inside, be prepared for a mess. A thin coating of craft varnish applied after wires are placed may help somewhat; check with the experts at your local craft store for advice.

- Use evergreens harvested from your own trees or from a nearby cut-your-own Christmas tree farm. Boughs that were cut at big, distant commercial operations in early November may have dried out so much that they won't absorb water.

Be selective in removing boughs from your trees. Where possible, take sections that need thinning or shaping.

Evergreen shrubs and trees that are ideal for holiday decorating because of their colorful needles, bright berries and woodsy fragrance include holly, cedar, pine, spruce, hemlock, fir and to a lesser extent, yews and junipers.

What to make? It might be something formal, elegant and entirely natural much like the wreaths fashioned today at Colonial Williamsburg from pine boughs, fresh lemons, pomegranates, pineapples and other materials available to residents in the late 1700s.

Or, it could be an arrangement that is spontaneous and simple and of the 1990s – perhaps a pickle crock filled with fragrant evergreen tips and interspersed with shiny red glass balls, pine cones and a short strand of miniature electric lights.

While there are plenty of decorating magazines and books with ideas, it can be just as much fun experimenting with different greens, containers, accessories and styles until you find something that works well for you and your decor.

Evergreens will hold needles longer if the end tips of the branches have a steady supply of fresh water. Saturated florist foam or shredded Styrofoam are both very useful as a means of anchoring the branches in a container, or the container can be filled with water and the branches arranged as you might informally arrange fresh flowers from the garden.

Before arranging, cut the end tip of the branch to aid water pickup. If florist foam is used, remove needles or leaves from the bottom inch or two of the branch to avoid creating an overly large hole in the foam when the branch is inserted.

If the greens are only needed for a few days, then a block of dry Styrofoam makes an excellent holder. In this case, the branches don't need recutting. Be sure to put something underneath the arrangement to protect surfaces from sticky and hard-to-remove sap that drips from the greens.

Select a few boughs from evergreen bushes in your yard to serve as a foundation for fresh holiday arrangements. Where possible, choose boughs that should be removed regardless of the holidays. Boughs extending over sidewalks or that don't contribute to the natural shape of the shrub are good candidates.

Sunflower seeds, fresh water spell happiness for birds

In a few weeks, as the holidays wind down, many of us will be ready to go on a diet. Some will go so far as to make a New Year's resolution to help make the conviction stick.

This isn't another of those awful dieting articles but it is about the diet that wild birds encounter this time of year, and some points to consider if you want to feed 'em.

Lots of people feed the birds. Some surveys put it as American's #2 pastime, right behind gardening. Like gardeners, there's no such thing as a typical bird feeding person. Some are fanatical about it, serving only choice black sunflower seed, accompanied by a fresh supply of water kept liquid over winter by an electric heater. Others consider bird feeding nothing more elaborate (or necessary) than throwing a piece of stale bread on the ground for the birds' next meal.

Based on a lot of reading and discussions with bird experts, here are some things I offer as you think about the birds in your backyard and how you might influence their diet this winter.

How do birds find the feeder you've set out for them? Do they see the food? Smell it? Sense its presence? Or simply stumble onto it? The general thinking is this: Birds are constantly on the watch for food and with their keen eyesight, can find it in many places. Your backyard feeder is simply one source for food. How attractive a feeding stop it becomes depends on the type of food offered, cleanliness, safety and water availability – all variables you can control. Here are details:

Type of food – Like people, birds have preferences. A researcher for the United States Fish and Wildlife Service studied the seed preference of 15 different birds – American goldfinch, chickadee, tufted titmouse, mourning dove, northern cardinal and others seen over winter in the Midwest.

The researcher ranked 21 different types of seed against one of two standard seeds (black-striped sunflower and white proso millet) and rated each on an attractiveness scale as high, moderate and low.

The winning seeds were black oil and black-striped sunflowers. Each scored a high attractiveness ranking among 12 different birds. Grey-striped and hulled sunflowers came in a distant second, with a high level of attractiveness to five birds. Thistle was highly attractive to only American goldfinch and the house sparrow.

Cleanliness – Some birds may be messy eaters, but they don't like seed that's become moldy because it's gotten wet or suet that's turned rancid from summer heat. The solution is to use suet only during cool months and to choose a feeder that keeps moisture from reaching the food. A rigorous scrubbing of the feeder every six months keeps things clean, too.

Water – A nearby source of water will encourage birds to stay near your feeder. Water is easy to provide year-around with a bird bath and an electric heater that keeps it ice-free during most months of the winter.

Safety – Shrubs or trees near the feeder give birds a place to land, rest and watch for predators. The berries and seeds of many trees and shrubs are also a welcome food source and in some cases, provide moisture as well. Provide shelter by locating your feeder within 15 feet of a sizable shrub or tree.

This style feeder is ideal for small birds and is one of the author's favorite's because of its sleek, no-nonsense design, steel construction and colorful finish (dark green, deep blue and berry red). The brand name is The Iron Silo and it sells for about $50. Look for it in garden centers and bird feeding supply stores.

Last-minute tips to help plants survive winter

This is the IF season in the landscape …

IF you've selected the right plants …

IF you've protected the tender ones …

IF you've kept plants healthy …

… then winter's wrath should have little, if any, harmful effects on the trees and shrubs in your yard. While it's too late in the year to make any sweeping changes to the health of your plants or the hospitality of the environment, a few small tasks may prove worthwhile providing you do them now.

Task #1: Protect young trees from serving as a food source for hungry rodents. They'll gnaw at the bark and layers underneath in the trunk area and by doing so, harm the tree's ability to move water and food. Rodents will do this underneath the snow. Protection is easy to provide. Wrap the trunk with tree wrap paper or surround it with a sleeve of foam pipe insulation or plastic drain tile. I prefer tile because it seems to be gnaw-proof and is wide enough to accommodate varying trunk diameters.

Task #2: Large-leaf rhododendron and holly bushes can lose a lot of water through their leaves over winter. Apply an anti-transpirant to reduce the loss. These materials are mixed with water and sprayed on the foliage to the point it drips off. Usually two applications 30 to 45 days apart provide adequate protection from the worst of winter wind and sun.

Check the label to be sure, but usually these materials are best applied at mid-day when it's sunny and the temperature is at least 40. If you have broadleaf evergreens and haven't sprayed them yet, be ready to do so the next time temperatures warm up.

Task #3: Some trees planted near the south or west wall of a building are at risk of bark splitting from the sun's warmth followed by evening cold. I've found this prevalent among some varieties of Japanese maple and Henry Lauder's walking stick (contorted filbert) and similar specimen trees with a gnarly branch structure.

The solution is easy and reasonably effective: Wrap the trunk where it makes sharp angles with tree wrap. The thick paper will moderate the hot-cold cycles of the day on the bark's surface and by doing so, reduce splitting.

Task #4: Lay in a supply of sandbox sand to sprinkle on icy walks and porches to improve traction. Sand won't harm shrubs and grass, as will some commercial de-icers, especially when they are over-applied. Sand is easy to clean up, inside and out. Look for it in bags in home centers or by the bucket at sand and gravel yards.

Task #5: Prune away branches from trees and shrubs that are likely to be damaged by weight from wet snow and ice. Better to prune them now, cleanly, then to have them ripped away from the trunk during a storm. It is not necessary to paint the end of the wound, but do make the cut a bit out from the trunk and at a slight angle. Check a pruning reference book for more details.

Plastic drain tile protects the trunk of this weeping cherry from rodents that might otherwise gnaw on it.

Go easy on food, water with houseplants

If a houseplant could talk, its first words once in your home might be: "I'll be okay if you leave me alone for a while."

Houseplants are a popular holiday gift and if you were lucky enough to receive one, here's a review of what to do and not do in the weeks ahead.

- Find a place to meet its need for light. Flowering plants and foliage plants with colorful leaves typically need more light than green foliage plants. The African violet and croton are examples of plants that need high light to do well.

A window facing unobstructed south or west usually provides sufficient light. Situate the plant as close to the window as possible, taking care that its leaves not touch the glass. Contact with very cold glass leads to frostbite, of sorts.

- No fertilizer – Your plant needs to get used to its new surroundings before stimulants like fertilizer are provided. Besides, it has some reserves from its days in the greenhouse.

- Little water –Your plant will need less water than normal during this period of adjustment. Water when the top inch of the soil is dry and discard any water that remains in the saucer after 30 minutes.

Experts concede that over-watering probably kills more houseplants than anything else. Joseph A. Cialone, Sr., a 30-year veteran of the foliage plant business, has worked out this formula that he says reduces watering frequency to once every three weeks:

Give water based on pot size. A 6-inch pot will take one pint of water every three weeks while a 14-inch pot needs 6 quarts. Other sizes take proportionally more or less water.

Even though the plant may wilt from dryness near the end of the three-week period, it will quickly recover when water is added and in a few months, adjust to the routine, Cialone said. He also recommends most plants be fed just once a year, in late spring and at half the recommended dose on the label.

Very vigorous plants can be fed four times annually, although Cialone does not believe that much fertilizer is really necessary. A Lake Worth, Fla., resident, he and his son raise thousands of specimen aglaonema (Chinese evergreen) plants for offices, malls and other big settings.

- Isolation – Keep the new plant away from other houseplants until you are sure it is pest-free. Look for hitchhiking insects on leaves, stems, stem tips and the soil before purchasing. A gentle shower in the bathtub will wash many pests from the foliage and stems, or use an insecticide formulated for houseplants. As with any garden chemical, please read and heed label instructions.

- Consider re-potting – Most houseplants do best when their root ball reaches throughout the inside of the pot. In a sense, they like to be "pot bound." When roots snake out of the bottom drainage holes or surface on the top of the soil, it is time to repot. Usually the next larger container provides the right fit.

Often it's a good idea to repot big foliage plants soon after they've been purchased if the pot appears small compared to the overall size of the plant. For best results, use a commercial houseplant potting soil blended for the type of plant in question.

This large houseplant needs repotting. One tell-tale sign is the presence of roots on the surface of the soil. Denise Williams, of Midland, Mich., checks the size of the existing pot and will re-pot it to a slightly larger container.

Entertaining kids bored during Christmas break

Somewhere between mastery of the latest electronic game and frustration with their friends not being around, parents can expect to hear a familiar lament from their kids: "I'm bored. What's there to do?"

What's to do takes many forms and from a gardener-parent perspective, here are some ideas to draw the kids out of their boredom and focus on the more primal things around the house.

While none of these ideas are likely to turn your child into a Luther Burbank, they'll at least occupy a youngster's time for a while.

Start a new plant – Poinsettias and Christmas cacti are easy for a youngster to clone by taking stem tip cuttings and rooting the shoots in moist sand or potting soil. Choose a fresh, young shoot and cut it off sharply from the mother plant between leaf breaks on the stem. With Christmas cacti, the cut should be between stem sections. Roots will develop within three weeks and the new plant can be potted in a larger pot. Enclosing the cutting in a plastic food bag will help it root faster by maintaining a favorably high level of humidity and temperature.

Collect dried pods – Forage through the backyard and public parks and wild areas for dried seed pods from milkweed, sweet gum, yucca, cattail and other autumn-seed bearing plants. If the autumn was mild, you may find many of these pods intact and well worth collecting for dried arrangements indoors.

New life for the Christmas tree – Put the tree outdoors to provide birds with shelter from weather and predators. Have the kids string popped popcorn and the cranberries that never got served into garlands that will provide food for the birds and color for humans watching inside. Use thick thread and heavy-duty sewing needles to make it easy for the youngsters.

Protein-packed bird snacks – Peanut butter and refined suet provide birds with a healthy diet. Put the kids to work smearing peanut butter between scales of pine cones, into empty bottle caps and similar receptacles that can be hung from trees outdoors. Plain, refined balls of suet sold by butchers and supermarkets can be made more nutritious by pressing bird seed into the fat.

Check out leftover garden seeds – Help your youngster better appreciate the miracle of seeds with a worthwhile experiment that will test the vitality of leftover garden seeds. Put 10 seeds from each packet within the folds of a moist paper towel and put it in a continually warm place, like on top of the refrigerator. A check of the towel after five days provides a good prediction of how many seeds will ultimately sprout in the garden next spring. Keep only packets that show a sprout rate of 60 percent or higher.

Burn off excess energy with a rake – If there's no snow, use youngsters' excess energy to rake up fallen leaves and other debris that have accumulated in the yard since what you thought was the final raking of the season. Chances are, this week will be a real blessing in that it provides one more opportunity to rake up leaves that could otherwise smother grass. The kids may not enjoy it, but the value of the task far outweighs listening to their grousing.

Leftover seeds any good? Try sprouting several in a moist paper towel kept warm to check for vigor. This is an excellent project to entertain youngsters for at least a few minutes over a span of several days.

Gardening Tidbits

Tender Care for Transplants

Getting annual flower and vegetable transplants off to a healthy start in the spring is easy. Here are some tips.

Buy only bushy, stocky plants. Avoid those with leggy stems and leaves spaced far apart, signs they haven't had enough light. Avoid plants with shrivelled leaves and stems. That's usually a signal they once dried out excessively. Choose young plants that are not in flower as they transplant better.

Once home, plant as soon as conditions are right. An overcast, calm afternoon with more of the same for the next day or two is ideal. Avoid planting on hot, bright and breezy mornings and afternoons. The sun and wind wring moisture from the plant quicker than its confused roots can replenish it. If bright conditions are to prevail, plant in the late afternoon when the sun has lost its punch.

If planting must be delayed beyond a day, keep the plants outdoors under filtered sunlight. Under a tree is fine.

Water immediately after planting. This provides moisture and closes the harmful air pockets that develop while planting. Water often enough to keep the soil evenly moist for at least the first week. This may mean watering every day while it is sunny and breezy. The plant may droop a bit during extremely hot and sunny weather, but a healthy plant will quickly bounce back with a few degrees of cooling.

Monthly feedings with a complete fertilizer (nitrogen, phosphorous and potassium) helps the plant reach its potential in flower or fruit production. Special blends are available for tomatoes and other crops. Don't overdo the feeding, though, or lush foliage instead of flowers or fruits will follow.

Houseplants Deserve Vacation, Too

Your houseplant will enjoy a summer vacation, too, especially if it's outdoors, under a tall shady tree. It will repay your efforts with healthy, robust growth.

Interested? If so, wait until all danger of frost has past, then put the plant in a very shady spot for the first five days. This may be under a tree or an overhang or may be on the north side. It should not receive any direct sunlight. Check the soil daily for water as it will dry out quickly in the fresh air.

After five days, move it to a little brighter spot, but not as bright as its ultimate destination. Keep it here another five days and continue to tend to its water needs. At the end of ten days, it will have adjusted to all the extra light and is ready to enjoy the summer in the spot you've picked for it. Hot, continual sun should be avoided for all but the most avid sunlovers. Hibiscus and bouganvillea are among the very few houseplants that like really hot sun.

The plant will need more water than when it was house-bound. Figure on doubling your efforts here. This doesn't mean water it twice as much. Check it twice as often and water as necessary.

Watch the plant for insects, especially in the heat of the summer when mites are happiest and most destructive. Check the undersides of leaves and new growth, since it is often the preferred meal of aphids and other sucking insects. If there is a problem, use the same houseplant insecticide used indoors, but be sure to read and follow the label instructions. Feed the plant with a houseplant fertilizer twice during the summer.

Three Popular Ways To Feed

It's no secret that a plant needs food to grow healthy. What's confusing is knowing the best way to get food to the plant. Here's a look at three popular ways.

Foliar feeding is easy and quick. Fertilizer in either dry or liquid form is mixed with water and applied to the leaves and base of the plant with a hose-end sprayer, watering can or bucket. The enriched solution is absorbed through the leaves and is carried in the sap stream to the roots where it goes to work. This is a good way to feed one-season plants, like flowers and vegetables.

Root feeding consists of putting food near the root zone where it will quickly dissolve and become available to the plant. One way is to punch holes in the soil with a heavy pipe and pour fertilizer in the hole. Another is to push fertilizer spikes into the soil. Yet another is with a root feeder, a device with a long, hollow spike that is inserted in the soil, through which liquid fertilizer flows. This is an excellent way to feed trees and shrubs.

Soil feeding involves working a measured amount of dry fertilizer into the soil surrounding the plant. While this is not practical for trees growing in lawns, it is a good technique for plants in flower and vegetable beds where the soil can be worked in early spring. It gives the plant a good, well-balanced meal since most formulations are designed to slowly release nutrients.

Fertilizer manufacturers have specific formulations for the different nutritional needs of popular landscape plants. It is wise to buy one to fit the plants that need feeding. As with any garden chemical, read and follow label instructions.

How To Drought-Proof a Landscape

Drought-proofing a landscape is easy and inexpensive. Here are some tips to help.

A two-inch layer of mulch around landscaped areas saves water, cools the soil and slows the growth of weeds. Natural mulch such as shredded bark, wood chips, pine needles, ground cocoa shells and similar materials look nice and improve the soil as they decompose.

Deliver water to the base of the plant or better yet, directly to its roots. It is wasteful to water shrubs or trees with an overhead sprinkler because much of the water is lost in the air or misdirected as droplets reach ground level. Use a bubbler on the end of the hose placed at the plant's base so only the immediate area is moistened. A root feeder is good because water is injected near the root zone.

Group plants with similar water needs. Shrubs like juniper, taxus and arborvitae require less water because their roots go deeper than many other plants, especially those that lose their leaves in the fall. Roses and geraniums take a lot of water.

Work a few shovels of sphagnum peat moss into the hole, especially if the native soil has a lot of clay or sand. The moss improves the ability of the existing soil to hold moisture at proper levels.

Plants signal water shortages by droopy branches, loss of leaves, slow growth and lack of flowers. Water and cultivate so these conditions do not occur because they usually indicate a plant is continually thirsty.

Tomatoes and Tubs and More

Vegetable gardening in containers rather than the garden is easy but takes attention to selecting the container, potting mix and variety.

A good homemade potting mix consists of equal parts garden soil, sphagnum peat moss and coarse sand or perlite. Sand is available where cement and gravel are sold. Look for peat and perlite at garden centers. Or, you can buy a mix blended for containers. I've had excellent results with store-bought container soils.

Choose a container with drainage holes or drill holes if there are none. Depth is important. A container 4 inches deep will grow lettuce, radishes and herbs, or 12 inches deep for miniature tomatoes and many varieties of carrots. Eight inches deep is plenty for peppers, cabbage and bush beans.

Bushel baskets, old tires, whiskey barrels, washtubs, livestock watering tubs and clay and plastic pots all work well and are available in a broad range of sizes.

Beans, beets, chard, eggplant, lettuce, peas, peppers, radishes, spinach, tomatoes and turnips grow well in containers, as do dwarf pumpkins, squash and watermelon.

This guide will help match vegetable to container:

Tub container, 2 to 5 gallons: Bush or vine beans, bush or vine cucumbers, eggplant, peppers, summer and winter squash, chard and tomatoes.

Plastic or clay pot, 8 to 12 inches across: Beans, beets, carrots, eggplant, lettuce, onions, peas, radishes, spinach, tomatoes and turnips.

Plastic or clay pot, 4 to 6 inches across: Lettuce, vining peas, spinach and chard.

Discarded tires: Dwarf or bush type pumpkins, squash or watermelon.

Move the container on the patio or balcony as needed to capture the most of the sun. Water carefully, mindful that clay or earthenware pots will dry out much quicker than plastic or other non-porous containers.

Getting Rid of Moss in Lawns

Moss in a lawn usually indicates poor soil aeration, poor drainage, low soil fertility, high soil acidity, heavy shade and high humidity. Not all conditions need be present for moss to flourish.

Fertility and acidity can be determined with a soil test and corrected, as results suggest. County extension offices usually offer help in arranging for a test and interpreting the results.

Aeration and drainage can be the result of foot traffic that has compacted the soil over time. Poor drainage can be an indication of a lawn built on a clay base, a very difficult condition to correct. Aeration can be improved by reducing traffic and loosening the soil by opening up tiny holes throughout the yard. This is best done by a professional with the proper power equipment.

Typically, a combination of chemical control, removal of dead moss plants and a fix of the environmental problem that prompted moss is usually necessary for a permanent solution.

Types of Roses Defined

Looking for a nice rose bush but confused about the different kinds and how to use them? Use this as a guide:

Hybrid tea – produce flowers with many petals and on long stems. Great for bud vases and arrangements. The classic rose.

Floribunda – produce lots of smaller flowers with fewer petals and the blossoms are clustered on short stems. Best used to provide garden color.

Grandiflora – usually, the best qualities of the hybrid tea and floribunda types – lots of shapely flowers that are good for cutting or garden color.

Landscape – new and exciting. They are winter-hardier and more resistant to disease and insects than other types and bloom throughout the summer. Good substitutes for forsythia, azalea, rhododendron, quince and other shrubs that bloom just once a year.

Miniature – typically grow less than 18 inches high with flowers less than two inches across. Leaves, blooms and thorns look like other types – but much, much smaller.

Climbing – grow long stems that can be tied to trellises, fences and other supports. There has not been much work in developing new varieties. Typically, a climber has one or two heavy blossom periods a season.

Shrub – are like our grandmothers grew. Most bloom but once or twice a season, are thorny, require little care and are wonderfully fragrant. Newer types are repeat bloomers.

A Summer Garden in the Window Well

Ever consider planting flowers in your window well? It's a perfect way to add color and excitement to an otherwise drab area.

A planter can be fashioned from a piece of half-inch plywood cut to fit the curve and size of the window well opening with plastic lawn edging to hold the soil in. Outdoor-rated plywood is best because it will last year after year. The edging is easily nailed or stapled in place, just inside the edges of the plywood. A six-inch-high strip is ideal, but four inches will do.

Before planting, check the fit and height of the planter. It may have to be raised several inches for the best viewing. Discarded bricks or lumber are sufficient for this.

Finally, fill the planter with a mix of equal parts garden soil and sphagnum peat moss and plant away. Choose plants that grow 6 to 15 inches tall. Good choices for sunny areas include marigolds, petunias, zinnias and geraniums and for shady spots, impatiens, wax begonias and vinca. Varieties that have a lot of small flowers rather than a few big flowers will look best.

Looking for a gift that is useful, affordable and sure to please? If so, consider this book.

It's a great gift for many occasions, such as:

- Housewarmings
- Anniversaries
- Hostess gift
- Birthdays
- As a "thank-you"
- Christmas and other holidays
- And many more

Additional copies are available from your bookseller.
Or, order direct from the publisher.

To order direct, send $12.95 for each copy ordered (Michigan residents please add 6 percent sales tax), plus $3 for first class postage and handling for the first copy and $1 for second and subsequent copies to:

From the Ground Up
Book Sales Division
4621 Congress Dr.
Midland, MI 48642-3911